Extraordinary courage, a crystal-clear vision, and a phenomenally fruitful evangelistic ministry in a pagan society. How did Saint Patrick do it? What were the 'secrets' of his success? Richard Roberts looks beneath the dynamics of his personal history and lived experience to examine the special features of Patrick's lasting spiritual impact. In a wide-ranging exploration of what a 'Saint Patrick inspired leadership-style' would look like today, this book invites us to consider how to penetrate an increasingly hostile culture, what kind of leaders the Church needs to develop and how we might measure our impact. Both the Church in the Western world and the secular culture around us could benefit from a few on-target Saint Patricks to inspire and guide us. Read this book all the way to its conclusion; it is full of good things.

-Stuart Bell, Assistant Bishop in the Anglican Convocation Europe

Hope from the life of Saint Patrick and the pen (heart) of Richard Roberts for those of us who trust that our mundane "long obedience in the same direction" bears fruit that lasts. What a breath of fresh air! In a time where the Church continues to be addicted to the corrosive leadership modes of power, impressiveness and relevance (Henri Nouwen), we have a clear and hopeful call that God can use the weak and pedestrian among us (like me) for His glory! I read it straight through because I couldn't put it down. This will become a standard text for leadership training in our community.

-Phil Dillingham, Priest Lake Christian Fellowship, Convenor of the Missional-Contemplative Roundtable (Middle Tennessee)

This book examines the leadership of Saint Patrick, one of the best-known leaders of the Celtic Church. Richard Roberts uses Patrick's own account of his life to examine several key issues that are very relevant for church leaders today. I highly recommend this book to anyone in leadership or to anyone who aspires to be a leader.

-Pastor Christer Borg, Church of Sweden (Lutheran)

I found this book thrilling and I read it at one sitting! What amazed me most was the author's ability to take a fifth century model for addressing a 21st century challenge. I had read several lives of St. Patrick, but I thought that this was an original manner of presenting the saint. The book clearly emphasises the vital importance of a Christian missionary incarnating himself/herself into a culture to be effective, just as Patrick 'incarnated' himself into the Celtic culture.

  -Archbishop Thomas Menamparampil, Guwahati, India

Saint Patrick: Resilience and Adaptability in Church Leadership *is a book with deep roots in the past, solid branches in the present, and offers a promise of rich fruit for the future. Roberts has carefully sifted through the literature on Patrick and 'Celtic Christianity,' presenting valuable wisdom and inspiration for Christian leaders in the coming generation. His treatment of the formation of leaders through our experience of hardship and interpersonal conflict alone is worth the price of the book. An excellent blend of respect for history, sensitivity to the Spirit, and practical communication.*

  -**Evan B. Howard**, author of A Guide to Christian Spiritual Formation: How Scripture, Spirit, Community, and Mission Shape our Souls

History teaches lessons if we will listen. Richard Roberts has listened well to the faith and practices of St. Patrick in a way that speaks to our own challenging times. The twin themes of resilience and adaptability, essentials for Christian leadership, are grounded in a profound trust in God that empowers such virtues. As Roberts suggests, St. Patrick's life is a parable that gives life and hope in the present whereby we might reimagine what church leadership means in the 21st century. Listen well to some interesting history, and, more importantly, embrace a type of leadership that cannot only survive challenges but flourish despite them.

  -**John Mark Hicks**, Retired Professor of Theology, Lipscomb University, TN

There is no dearth of books dedicated to the subject of leadership and no fewer than 407 colleges and universities in the United States, both Christian and secular, offer degrees or classes on leadership. Many of these 'Schools of Leadership' were established only in the last 25-30 years. Men and women spend thousands of dollars attending these schools, not to mention those who spend similar amounts of money to attend lectures, or buy books, on leadership offered by such experts as John Maxwell. So, why another book on leadership? Dr Richard J. Roberts, retired physician and House Church leader in the UK, offers a unique take on Christian leadership by looking at the lives of Celtic saints, such as St. Patrick of Ireland, to see if we, in the 21st century can glean insights from the lives of these men and women.

Saint Patrick: Resilience and Adaptability in Church Leadership *is the first volume in a series of books that plans on addressing the same subject of leadership in the life and ministries of St. Columba and Finnian. In the book's Foreword, Dr Gordon Robertson, President of the Christian Broadcasting network and Chancellor of Regent University in Virginia Beach, Virginia, writes that Richard Roberts '…skilfully unpacks key themes from Patrick's life that transcend the boundaries of time and culture. We journey through the annals of Patrick's experiences, guided by a desire to distil the essence of his leadership.' Gordon Robertson goes on to state what were the hallmarks of Patrick's leadership; he received a 'clear divine calling', his 'openness to the Spirit, grounding in the Word, adept navigation of conflicts and unyielding confidence in God.'*

I can happily recommend this insightful volume to anyone who wants to explore how the great saints of the past can still impact our lives today, for 'Their voice have gone out through all the earth, and their words to the end of the world' (Psalm 19:4).

-The Very Reverend Timothy Cremeens, PhD, Greek Orthodox Archdiocese of North America and member of the Leadership Committee of the Ecumenical Forum

REIMAGINING CHURCH LEADERSHIP

Saint Patrick
Resilience & Adaptability
in Church Leadership

Dr Richard J Roberts

 Finnian Press

Copyright © 2024 Dr Richard John Roberts

All rights reserved. This book or any portion thereof may not be reproduced or used in any manner whatsoever without the express written permission of the author except for the use of brief quotations in a book review.

Quotations from Patrick's writings are from Fr Padraig McCarthy's translation in: Anthony Harvey and Franz Fischer (eds), *The St Patrick's Confessio Hypertext Stack* (Dublin: Royal Irish Academy), online as www.confessio.ie since September 2011. Used by permission.

Unless otherwise indicated, all Scripture quotations are from The Holy Bible, English Standard Version® (ESV®), copyright © 2001 by Crossway, a publishing ministry of Good News Publishers. Used by permission. All rights reserved.

ISBN eBook 978-1-8384190-7-3
ISBN Print   978-1-8384190-8-0

Finnian Press,
Beaminster,
Dorset.

Contents

Acknowledgements I
Foreword III
Introduction 1

LIVING IN TIMES OF DISCONTINUOUS CHANGE 5
Context 6
Crisis 17

LEADERSHIP & CALLING 25
Call 26
Conflict 34

COURAGE TO LEAD 45
Confidence 46
Commission 57

CONTEMPORARY LEADERSHIP & SAINT PATRICK 67
Culture 68
Cul-de-sacs 80

FINAL THOUGHTS 91
Culmination 92
Conclusion 102
Terminology 115
Further Reading 119
About the Author 125

Acknowledgements

Many people have helped, directly and indirectly, in the creation of this book. My wife, Norma, put up with my being ensconced in the study to write. She also worked tirelessly to edit the manuscript and made important suggestions about the content. Simon and Jen Roberts employed both artistic and graphic design skills to create a pleasing cover.[1]

A weekend spent at Waverley Abbey in discussion with fellow writers Evan B Howard, Jill Weber, Tim Otto, Jason Clark and Clive Orchard was particularly helpful in honing my ideas. I am also especially grateful to Gordon Robertson for his excellent foreword. Several friends have reviewed or made comments on the manuscript, including David Lawrence, Clive Orchard, Bob Stradling and Matt Smith. Malcolm Dunn's final edit and attention to detail was invaluable.

Fr Padraig McCarthy generously gave permission to quote extensively from his translation of source documents.

Last but not least, I would like to thank my church family at The Meeting Place, particularly those who regularly pray for me and whose support has been a great encouragement. You have helped me reimagine what church and leadership might look like in the 21st century.

---

[1] www.simonroberts.co.uk

Foreword

In the ever-shifting landscape of contemporary Christian leadership, the journey of leading a church, home group, or any Christian organization demands an inspired approach. Dr Richard J Roberts takes us on a transformative exploration in *Saint Patrick: Resilience & Adaptability in Church Leadership*, inviting us to learn insights from the resilient leadership of one of the most iconic figures in the history of the Church.

As we embark on this intellectual and spiritual odyssey, Dr Roberts illuminates the parallels between the complexities faced by leaders today and the tumultuous era in which Saint Patrick navigated his remarkable ministry. The echoes of societal shifts and the marginalization of the Church resonate across the ages, compelling us to confront the confusion that marks our own contemporary landscape.

In the following pages, Dr Roberts artfully weaves together scholarly depth and a light touch, skilfully unpacking key themes drawn from Patrick's life that transcend the boundaries of time and culture. We journey through the annals of Patrick's experiences, guided by a desire to distil the essence of his leadership—his clear divine calling, openness to the Spirit, grounding in the Word, adept navigation of conflicts, and unyielding confidence in God.

At the heart of this exploration is the conviction that Patrick's narrative serves as more than a historical account—it is a living parable, a reservoir of wisdom that can guide and inspire leaders grappling with the challenges of our time. The intention is not to prescribe a rigid blueprint for leadership but to offer a thoughtful resource that will spark a reimagining of servant leadership.

Saint Patrick: Resilience & Adaptability in Church Leadership is the inaugural volume in a series that promises to be an enriching journey into the lives of various Celtic Saints such as Columba and Finnian. Each saint, a distinct beacon of inspiration, will provide unique perspectives on ways of being for today's church leaders. Through this series, Dr Roberts invites us to glean insights from these luminaries, shaping a comprehensive tapestry of leadership wisdom drawn from the wellspring of Celtic Christianity.

As you embark on this literary voyage, you will find not only a historical exploration but a guidebook for navigating the uncharted waters of leadership in our times. Dr Roberts masterfully bridges the ancient and the contemporary, inviting leaders to draw from the well of Patrick's experiences, allowing the spirit of innovation and resilience to infuse their own leadership narratives.

May *Saint Patrick: Resilience & Adaptability in Church Leadership* be a source of inspiration, provoking thoughtful reflection and fostering a renewed sense of purpose for leaders seeking to lead with fidelity and fruitfulness amid the uncertainties of our changing world. May we all benefit from the wisdom of St. Patrick and the blessing of the prayer known as *St. Patrick's Breastplate*:

> Christ with me,
> Christ before me,
> Christ behind me,
> Christ in me,
> Christ beneath me,
> Christ above me,

Foreword

Christ on my right,
Christ on my left,
Christ when I lie down,
Christ when I sit down,
Christ when I arise,
Christ in the heart of every man who thinks of me,
Christ in the mouth of everyone who speaks of me,
Christ in every eye that sees me,
Christ in every ear that hears me.

Gordon Robertson
President of the Christian Broadcasting Network
Chancellor of Regent University

Introduction

Finally settling upon the right words or appropriate phrase to use as a book title is a challenging task as there are usually a considerable number of suitable alternatives which aptly describe the content. One possibility for this book was *Saint Patrick: A Life Interrupted*, since not only was Patrick's life profoundly affected by major changes in the cultural, political, and religious landscape of his land of origin, but also his early privileged upbringing was severely disrupted at the age of 16 by being abducted to Ireland as a slave. Not only that, but God seriously interrupted any trajectory he might have envisaged, as well as any plans he might personally have had, by subsequently calling him to Christian ministry and discipleship, going on to shape his future as a missionary and leader in what was for him a very alien culture and country.

Today, we too similarly face far-reaching cultural, political and religious changes as well as profound environmental changes, most way beyond our control. Our personal lives are also, of course, from time to time interrupted by unforeseen, often unwelcome, events but, like Patrick, we are called by God to engage with ministry, mission, and leadership in less-than-ideal, often adverse, circumstances. This book is written in the hope that Patrick's story, although circumstantially quite different from ours, will be a source of inspiration to help us navigate the many diverse challenges and opportunities which our particular and unique landscape and time presents. Those themes which characterised Patrick's setting and his ministry have resonances with our own situation in the West. To use a musical analogy, while the melody of Patrick's life was completely different from our own and the words we are called to sing are also not the same, the baseline is not only clearly discernible but may well resonate deeply with us.

Accordingly, a number of themes from the life of St Patrick are outlined to highlight certain issues surrounding leadership in any age. Patrick's life poses questions about many of the approaches we adopt as we struggle with the task of leadership today and his example helps us in our deliberations as we seek to reflect on and evaluate contemporary models of leadership.

* * * * * * * *

In attempting to outline the contours of Patrick's life, I have drawn upon reliable scholarly sources, particularly relying on the two documents accepted as coming from the hand of Patrick himself, his *Confession* and *Letter to the Soldiers of Coroticus*. There have been several interpretations of Patrick's life, some challenging the previous consensus. There is, for example, the Two Patricks Theory which suggests that early biographers conflated the stories of two separate people to construct one single narrative – a composite Patrick. Others suggest that he wasn't actually abducted by raiders and taken into slavery, but rather that he had actually chosen to go to Ireland (perhaps as an early form of a gap year).

I follow the traditional view, although not uncritically, that we can take his account at face value. I have sought to avoid too much wishful or romanticised thinking, a criticism levelled at much written about the Celts, in the hope that the relevance of Patrick's ministry for today, as well as the inspiration we might draw from his life and God's dealings with him, are apparent. Of course, while we remember that the accounts of Patrick's life and his writings are not Scripture, his story provides us with an incredible example of God using someone, in all their weakness and human frailty, to His greater glory.

His story also brings into focus certain aspects of good leadership that we see reflected in the lives of Jesus, Paul and many other biblical figures. I have emphasised those aspects of his ministry that strike me as being most relevant to leadership today and, therefore, the selection of topics or themes has been somewhat subjective. Others may highlight different aspects of Patrick's life.

* * * * * * * *

The book is divided into five sections:

- The first explores the cultural and historical backdrop to Patrick's life and ministry. Some of this is not, strictly speaking, about Patrick himself but it does help us to appreciate the challenges he (and his contemporaries) faced, as well as providing a way of reflecting on our own situation.

- The second section looks at the way in which God's call to Patrick gave shape to his ministry and created the unique contours of his life as a missionary to Ireland. His was not an easy path, and it required a strong sense of God's leading so that he could embrace the risk and face the opposition encountered as he pursued his calling.

- The third section explores the source of Patrick's confidence in God and in what ways and in what circumstances his example might motivate us to have a similar confidence today.

- The fourth section focuses on important issues for Christian leaders today. Some of the themes explored earlier in the book are examined in greater detail, especially as they are relevant to our situation in the West.
- The final section evaluates the outcome of Patrick's ministry and how, using his example, we might reimagine church leadership today.

Saint Patrick: Resilience & Adaptability in Church Leadership is the first in a short series of books examining selected Celtic saints and the themes emerging from the accounts of their lives. Once their stories capture our imaginations, we see new possibilities for the Church and our place within it. They can *inspire* us and provide the opportunity for a creative *reimagining* of a possible future, including reimagining the way in which leadership might be outworked.[2] Patrick's story is one example of how God can shape and use imperfect people in desperate circumstances, and this raises the possibility that He might do the same with us in our day. Such a possibility renders our situation as being one of hope rather than of despair.

---

[2] The concept of reimagining the future is central to Walter Brueggemann's *Prophetic Imagination*. Minneapolis, Fortress Press, 2001.

PART 1
LIVING IN TIMES OF DISCONTINUOUS CHANGE

1

Context

Each year on March 17th - the date, according to tradition, of St Patrick's death - the Chicago River is dyed green for the benefit of the Irish American population (and the chance, no doubt, to make a buck!) The dish of corned beef and cabbage is served, and people wear green. There are marches with banners and pipe bands as people celebrate their heritage in places such as Boston and New York. Worldwide, draught Guinness is consumed in large quantities – 13 million pints by some estimates - and small bands of fiddle, mandolin and squeezebox players are to be heard live or piped in bars. Meanwhile, in Australia, the Sydney Opera House is illuminated in green, alongside marches also taking place at various times in many other cities around the world.

This has echoes of the St Patrick who drove snakes from Ireland (there never were any there in the first place) and the Patrick who, according to legend, used the shamrock to teach about the Trinity (most probably he didn't). In this version of Patrick, he is placed alongside leprechauns and Irish dancing as being quintessentially Irish. Except, of course, he wasn't. He may even have been a Latin-speaking Welshman!

Patrick, likely to have been born at the end of the 4th century, was a near contemporary of Augustine of Hippo, the famous North African theologian (and not to be confused with the later archbishop of Canterbury). Although Patrick and

Augustine of Hippo would not have met, they each produced autobiographies, called *Confessions*. As the earliest autobiographies known, rather than being confessions of sin, their memoirs were confessions of their faith, tracing the hand of God in their lives. These two men recorded their testimonies to His faithfulness and providential intervention at various points in their experience to create 'spiritual biographies'. Patrick's was probably written towards the end of his life.

The other accounts of Patrick's life, such as Muirchu's 7th century biography, rather than being an accurate record of events, were written much later, centuries after Patrick's death, and are generally considered unreliable, being peppered with details designed to bolster the reputation of 'their saint' and often with the aim of asserting the superiority of their particular branch of the Irish Church. These accounts, which also tend to portray a very romanticised view of Patrick's life and ministry, are in stark contrast to Patrick's own record which outlines a hard and lonely path, beginning with his captivity and enslavement as a teenager.

Perhaps, however, this contrast between the idealised version of Christian ministry and the reality which we actually experience can encourage us when church life turns out to be harder than we might wish. The biblical record and the most accurate accounts of the lives of the saints remind us that responding to God inevitably involves encountering and overcoming challenges. Difficulties do not necessarily signal that we are approaching ministry in the wrong way.

Romano-British Life

Patrick was 'Romano-British' – genetically a Briton but culturally Roman. His world was one of mosaic floors, learning Latin and wearing togas, with Christianity dominating in both private and public life (at least in the towns). The Roman presence in Britain formed the backdrop to Patrick's early life, providing a measure of stability. Roman legions had defended her borders against hostile forces in the North, Irish raiders from the West, and warlike tribes from the continent of Europe. The Roman Empire was characterised by its famous roads, villas with underfloor central heating and, wherever Rome held sway, its common language, Latin, was spoken by the elites. Since Constantine's adherence to Christianity in 312 AD the Empire had been increasingly 'Christianised' - to the point where some, the Desert Fathers and Mothers, feeling that Christianity had been domesticated and compromised, decided to flee to the desert to live a simple but radical life of discipleship.

The world in which Patrick was born was very different from our own, one important difference being the central role that religion played in framing everyday life. As one author points out, 'We recite the same creed, but our expectation of how believing involves us in the whole structure of reality is radically different'.[3] It is difficult for us in a secularised society to appreciate how pervasive the influence of religion was at that time. Meaning for citizens of the Empire was to be found in a whole variety of religions on offer, including the newer 'mystery religions' and the worship of ancient gods, as well as in Christianity. A minority of Roman citizens turned to philosophy rather than to religion, notably the Stoic emperor Marcus Aurelius whose *Meditations* continue to prove popular, but, for the vast majority of people in Patrick's day, it was the gods or God who provided the significant reference points.

This was unlike present times in the secular West where there are alternative, more material, explanations for reality, especially those of science, with its quest to comprehend the

---

[3] Thomas O'Loughlin, *Saint Patrick: The Man and his Work.* London, SPCK, 1999, p.3.

origin and configuration of all things. Even those of us who adhere to a Christian worldview are very likely also to accept many of the tenets of modern science as well as frameworks for understanding human behaviour drawn from social sciences, psychology and sociology, with modern medicine explaining what has gone wrong with our bodies and minds. Even if, like me, we believe in a spiritual dimension to life, including the personal reality of evil and the availability of the power of the Holy Spirit, our explanation for the events around us will, in all probability, also take science, psychology, etc into account.

In the days of the Roman Empire, however, religion was centre stage. Christianity had taken a firm hold in Roman Britain, albeit mainly in larger settlements, while the persistence of pagan shrines in rural areas suggests that outside these centres of population most people remained steeped in the old religion of their ancestors.

Instability

In 410 AD the arrival of Germanic tribes at the gates of Rome triggered the complete retreat of the legions from the outskirts of the Empire, including from Britain. However, it appears that the basic structures of Roman society remained intact for many years after the legions had withdrawn, and, initially, life for most Britons would have continued as normal. The recently excavated villa at Chedworth in Gloucestershire (UK) had a mosaic floor which was laid around 424 AD. This was after the withdrawal of the legions and suggests that the Roman way of life continued in the West for a period of time.[4]

The stability of being a Roman colony had actually begun to be eroded even prior to the complete withdrawal that occurred

---

[4] See: https://www.thehistoryblog.com/archives/60220 accessed 14.01.24.

in 410 AD. In order to deal with the growing threat from the Germanic tribes, several legions had earlier been recalled to Italy in order to defend their homeland. In the absence of the protection of an empire, the gradual infiltration of more hostile forces led to change. By the time of Patrick's birth at the end of the fourth century, the Roman legions had already withdrawn from the northern and western edges of Britain (where very probably Patrick himself had lived), leaving her inhabitants relatively unprotected from marauding neighbours, including the Picts from present-day Scotland and the Scoti from Ireland. The term Scoti meant either 'sea rovers' or 'men of darkness'. In other words, they were pirates and the sort of people who formed the basis of tales told by mothers to keep their children from straying into forbidden territory!

Britain was now in the hands of regional rulers, who increasingly were unable to repel these marauding slavers and looters. In the first half of the 5th century these rulers began to employ Angles and Saxons from the near continent as a form of private army. This course of action proved to be unwise as the Saxon 'guests', who had initially been invited to come to Britain as a paid security force against these incursions, exploited the power vacuum and established their own independent kingdoms in the South. This dynamic added to the developing crisis, as civil order was gradually eroded and many cities and homes, including the many sophisticated Roman-style villas, with their sewers and underfloor heating, were eventually abandoned. (It would be 1,400 years before sewers were re-established!)

While the version of events portraying the Anglo-Saxons as an invading hoard may be factual, it is also possible that the 'invasion' was less dramatic and was more like a gradual infiltration of settlers whose paganism, artistry and customs increasingly appealed to the rural Britons - much as, in our day, eastern mysticism and New Age beliefs have become more mainstream through a process of gradual assimilation.

As far as the Church was concerned, once the Saxons were well established in Britain, certainly before the time of Patrick's death, Christianity would become increasingly confined to the western and northern regions of the country and elsewhere a resurgent paganism was in the ascendant. Remote and inaccessible places, such as Wales, in fact did remarkably well in surviving as pockets of Christian culture. It was not until the much later arrival of Augustine (of Canterbury) that any major re-evangelisation of central southern Britain occurred.

Decline

Patrick was born at the beginning of this period of unforeseen and uncontrollable change for the inhabitants of Britain. It is likely that he was living in a region that would over several decades become one of several Christian enclaves. He would have been absent in Ireland at this time when many such changes reached their climax, and he may not have observed first-hand the degradation of the country which, as one prominent scholar puts it, had 'slipped back into conditions more brutally simplified than the Iron Age societies that had preceded the coming of the Romans'.[5]

According to the Venerable Bede, stability gave way to instability, predictability to confusion and order to chaos: 'Britain… lay wholly exposed to plunderers… the Irish from the West and the Picts from the North'.[6] Bede was writing several centuries after the events described and it is more likely that change was, in fact, much more gradual than he had thought.

---

[5] Peter Brown, *The Rise of Western Christendom.* Oxford, Blackwell, 2003, p.126.

[6] Bede, The Ecclesiastical History of the English People. Oxford, OUP, 2008, Chapter 12.

Yet for those who remained true to the Christian faith, the decades that followed Rome's withdrawal would have been a shocking and traumatic time of transition, with an increasing threat from hostile forces, and eventually Christians would find themselves to be a religious minority.

It was probably unimaginable to people living at the height of Rome's rule that there could be a collapse of such a stable civilisation which had actually existed for centuries. The extensive system of Roman roads, powerful armies, freedoms of trade and a judicial system all hugely benefitted citizens (though not, of course, slaves and others at the bottom of society in Britain). The collapse of the empire was perhaps just as unthinkable as the thought that conceivably our own civilisation could give way to a new chaotic order. The accompanying marginalisation of the Church could not, in such circumstances, be resisted and an appeal that was based on history, reason or its benefits for civil order would have had no influence on those now in power. These uncomfortable facts had to be faced. Life was becoming much less certain and relying on God became more challenging in certain respects but, as is the case in our day, even more necessary.

Missiologists Roxburgh and Romanuck use the phrase 'massive discontinuous change' to describe these and other such profoundly disorientating experiences and events. The new situation arising from such change bears little relationship to the past state of affairs – it is, therefore, 'discontinuous' with what has gone before.[7] Despite being separated by hundreds of years, there are definite parallels with our own time. We in the West also live in a period of profound cultural change and the Church no longer occupies the privileged position in society that it once enjoyed. This is especially the case in

---

[7] Alan Roxburgh and Fred Romanuck, *The Missional Leader: Equipping Your Church to Reach a Changing World.* San Francisco, Jossey-Bass, 2006.

Europe, where the Church's role has largely been relegated to ceremonial events. Active Christian faith is now almost a minority pursuit. The same is increasingly true in North America, albeit to a lesser extent in some states, and Christian values and beliefs are frequently regarded by secular powers as being outmoded or problematic.

The Dark Ages

This period of time, from the 5th to the 11th centuries, is referred to as the 'Dark Ages', a term which latterly has fallen out of favour. For part of the 6th century, however, it was literally dark since volcanic ash from Iceland darkened the sun, causing crops to fail for a period of successive years. People starved and plague broke out. This upheaval in society was the backdrop to much of the story of the Celtic Church, just as the environmental crisis and its increasingly dramatic effects form the backdrop to our own story. Even a century before this volcanic eruption, as Thomas O'Loughlin notes, Patrick believed the world was in its last days and he linked his mission with the imminent return of Christ.[8] It was into this dark and threatening age that Patrick was thrust. We shall see that Patrick's faith was based on the certainty of the final triumph of God at the end of the Age, although in no way was this triumphalism (when we naively believe that our prayers and strident declarations of faith will instantly overcome any and every obstacle of life encountered).

Yet life would become even darker for the teenage Patrick when he was transported to Ireland and sold into what he quite naturally assumed would be lifelong slavery.[9] This unfamiliar and forbidding land was ruled over by fierce pagan warrior-

---

[8] O'Loughlin (1999), p.42-7.

[9] This was probably sometime around 405 AD.

kings with their druid advisors. He felt that he had been plunged into an environment where his security was stripped away: 'It was among foreigners that it was seen how little I was'.[10]

Patrick's Story in Brief

Eventually, Patrick, one of the original evangelists and church planters in Ireland, became known as the Apostle to the Irish. Having first arrived in Ireland as a slave he later returned as a missionary bishop. His story illustrates the fact that God was at work even in dire personal circumstances and that the Dark Ages, which followed the collapse of the Roman Empire was, paradoxically, a time of mission and growth in certain regions.

St Patrick, Patricius in Latin, had been born into a well-to-do religious family sometime around 390 AD. His father was a town councillor (senator) who owned a small estate, so his early life would have been relatively privileged. Although Patrick himself identified his place of birth as Bannavem Taburniae, there is uncertainty as to its location, with some favouring Wales, others Scotland, and yet others, Cumbria in the north of England. Very probably, Bannavem Taburniae was located on the western fringes of Britain, since these areas were easily accessible to the pirate-raiders who plied their trade in Ireland and had been responsible for capturing the young Patrick.

However, this relatively settled existence for Patrick was to become increasingly unstable and insecure when, completely unexpectedly, he was captured by marauding pirates and transported to Ireland. Ireland was a slave economy where cattle, rather than money, was the currency. Slave girls were, however, prized even more highly than cattle and some goods

---

[10] *Confessio* 1

were priced in terms of their equivalent value. Many of the slaves were in fact Christians, and this is probably how the faith first came to the shores of Ireland.[11] Irish warrior-kings usually had several wives and, in addition, took slave concubines so that they could father large ruling clans. Under their rule were peasant farmers but the lowest rung in society consisted of slaves like Patrick who had been purchased from the pirate-raiders. Slaves expected to end their days in hardship and heavy labour and Patrick's owner put him to work herding sheep and pigs on the wild Atlantic coast of County Mayo. Despite a secure upbringing in a well-to-do family, he had ended up as a shepherd, an unexpected and unlikely occupation for someone of his social standing of origin.

Slavery is grim in any situation and County Mayo would have been an undesirable place in which to have been a slave. The climate is inhospitable since, on average, it rains there more than 60% of the time. As a child, my wife spent family holidays near Ireland's west coast. She recalls being rowed across a lake (in the driving rain), a pony and trap ride (in the rain) as well as touring amidst beautiful rolling hills and valleys (in the mist). No wonder Patrick resorted to prayer, imploring God to rescue him from his plight and the result was that his 'faith grew and [his] spirit was moved...'[12] His love for God and his fear of Him grew in adversity. When God finally answered his prayers, after six years in captivity, his prayers would by then have numbered tens of thousands. Remarkably, after six years, Patrick, under God's guidance, managed to escape and was able to return to his homeland.

Despite the fact that his father was a deacon and his grandfather a priest, Patrick had not taken faith very seriously

---

[11] Christian traders may also have settled in Ireland and formed part of the Church there.

[12] *Confessio* 16

as he grew up, even with having had a very solid upbringing in the Roman Church of his day.[13] Prior to his captivity he appears to have been only nominally Christian, but during his time in slavery his stance changed and faith became increasingly central to his existence.

After many years, years largely shrouded in mystery, Patrick returned to the land of his captivity as a missionary and had great success, mainly in the northwest of Ireland. The trigger for his return was a dream in which he believed the voice of the Spirit was calling him back to Ireland. The actual date of his death is uncertain but was sometime between the early 460s and the 490s AD. Despite a difficult start, Patrick eventually came to influence a wide variety of people, ranging from local kings to slaves, suggesting that there was something about his life that was hugely attractive to others.

---

[13] Married priests were acceptable in the Church in Patrick's day.

2
Crisis

While it is likely that those on the western fringes of Britain had always been subject to occasional Irish raiding parties seeking plunder and slaves, the situation would worsen as the Roman legions withdrew, and Patrick was taken captive. The change in his circumstances had been sudden, unpredictable and deeply shocking, giving Patrick little or no sense of continuity with his former life up to that point.

Patrick's subsequent call to mission, which we will examine in detail later, was set against this backdrop and, once he had returned to Ireland as a missionary bishop, it would take him into possibly even more challenging circumstances. We, of course, with the benefit of hindsight, know the end of the story. His evangelism in Ireland eventually resulted in 'reverse mission' as Irish monks returned to Patrick's shores and contributed to the re-evangelisation of western Britain and present-day Scotland. But Patrick himself knew none of these things.

Eugene Peterson, one of my favourite authors, coined the phrase 'the mystery and the mess' to describe the paradoxical experience of God being present in the midst of life, even in and despite all its human frailty, sin, chaos and confusion. This phrase aptly describes Patrick's life and ministry. The circumstances of his life resulted in experiences of profound *disorientation* in many areas, but also, perhaps paradoxically, these very experiences turned out to be the context which God could actually use to *reorientate* him, form his character and deepen his trust.

Captivity

Patrick's experience of slavery in Ireland was hugely disorientating and plunged him into great uncertainty, yet this horrifically disturbing and deeply upsetting experience would form the basis for his ministry and develop his lifelong trust in God. This formative though desolate period of his life resulted in fervent prayer born out of desperation:

> After I arrived in Ireland, I tended sheep every day, and I prayed frequently during the day. ... so that in one day I would pray up to one hundred times, and at night perhaps the same.[14]

Elizabeth Reese suggests that in adopting the practice of frequent prayer Patrick 'became converted to the monastic way'.[15] While this might possibly be overstating the case, we can certainly see similarities between Patrick's situation and that of solitary monks in the Egyptian desert with their life of ongoing and constant work and prayer. It was in this context of adversity that Patrick, with no ideas or strategies of his own to rely upon, learned to hear the voice of God and began to respond to His leading. This listening stance was the foundation not just for his escape from slavery but for his eventual return to Ireland.

The relevance of combining prayer and listening for the voice of the Spirit cries out to leadership today as we too face

---

[14] *Confessio* 16
[15] Elizabeth Reese, *A Dictionary of Celtic Saints*. Stroud, The History Press, 2012, p.126.

major upheavals in both the Church and society around us. A question to ask ourselves in such circumstances is where we might actually place our trust – is it in our own abilities, wisdom and experience, or is it primarily in the God who hears and responds to our cries (Exodus 3:7)? Have we learned to discern the voice of the Spirit, or do we look to our own ingenuity and strength to find our way ahead?

The story of Patrick reminds us, as does the story of God's people in the Bible, that He is often at work on the margins rather than in the centres of ecclesiastical or political power. This is the case whether we look at slaves in Egypt or a baby born in a stable and it was certainly true in the case of Patrick.

Liminality

The sociologist Victor Turner coined the term 'liminality' to describe disorientating situations, such as Patrick's, in which old certainties are no longer operative.[16] Liminality is experienced when we are on the threshold between a secure past and an uncertain future. The experience of liminality is evocatively described by W B Yeats in his poem *The Second Coming*, written in the aftermath of the First World War:

> Things fall apart; the centre cannot hold;
> Mere anarchy is loosed upon the world,
> The blood-dimmed tide is loosed, and everywhere
> the ceremony of innocence is drowned...

'Liminality' not only describes the slowly developing crisis in Britain as the legions began to withdraw and the future became increasingly uncertain: it was also to be an ongoing and

---

[16] For helpful insights into the value of liminal experiences see Alan Hirsch, *The Forgotten Ways: Reactivating the Missional Church*. Grand Rapids, Brazos Press, 2006, chapter 8.

profoundly difficult experience for Patrick personally once he was taken into slavery in a strange alien culture on the edge of the then known world. He was, like Robinson Crusoe, separated from all he had known, stranded in an unfamiliar and unmapped new world. Although Patrick was later to willingly embrace uncertainty as part and parcel of his call to return to Ireland, he had an enduring sense of being in a liminal space on the edge of all things. As Thomas O'Loughlin describes, he felt that he was at the ends of the earth; on the edge of society; and at the end of time.[17]

Liminality provides the setting for most popular action-adventure movies, perhaps because it resonates with the sense of unease that we in the West have concerning the bewildering and unstable world in which we find ourselves. We currently face changing cultural mores, the perceived political threat from China, Russia and radical Islamic states, unknown threats involving the misuse of technology, the likelihood of future pandemics and the use of biological warfare, as well as seismic catastrophic climate change.

The film *The Bourne Identity* is gripping because it describes a quest which leads the hero beyond the boundaries which normally make him feel secure. The elements of this liminal experience for him include confusion as to what is going on and not knowing whom he can trust. He experiences the loss of the usual networks of friends and colleagues upon which he can normally depend (although true to the stereotypical action-movie, Jason Bourne finds a similarly disorientated companion to join him in his quest).

Perhaps this genre of film is popular because it helps us to connect to any sense we may have that we too are on an impossible quest, out of our depth, running to keep up and trying desperately to keep hope alive. This may well be an

---

[17] O'Loughlin (1999), pps.42-7.

experience common to many in Western society, including even those in church leadership. Our instinctive response is to try to get things back to how they were, back to the old 'normal', but this, sadly, is both futile and misguided. Liminal situations, however, do demand more of us than simply passively observing or commenting on the way things have become. They require an active response.

Finding Our Way

The story of Patrick's life can act as inspiration for a different approach to leadership, one that embraces powerlessness and is, therefore, not reliant on the quest to gain mastery over every challenging situation in which we find ourselves. In a similar vein, missiologist Alan Roxburgh suggests several productive ways in which we can choose to act in our 'strange new world'. Rather than reacting defensively we can actually move out of secure established positions; we can let go of position and status and we can learn ourselves how to excel in transitional situations because there are no real experts to fall back upon.[18] Patrick took this route, not initially out of choice but out of necessity, for the sake of survival. In addition to Roxburgh's thought-provoking advice, Patrick's example highlights the vital place of prayer, combined with an openness to the Spirit, in liminal situations.

When we come to the saints explored in this short series of books, we find few if any magic bullets and a relative dearth of practical problem-solving techniques. Although there were familiar patterns of ministry, these were often based on seeking to personally know and serve God, rather than being off-the-peg models for leadership success.

---

[18] Alan Roxburgh, *The Sky is Falling: Leaders Lost in Transition*. Eagle, ID, ACI Publishing, 2005, p.110.

Patrick's own testimony was that both his formation and call to leadership were wholly initiated by the God who drove him further and further into liminal situations. Perhaps we too are able to discern the hand of God even in times of difficulty when we feel out of our depth. God taught Patrick not just to survive but to thrive in places of uncertainty, as he learned to *listen* to the voice of the Spirit.

Learning to Listen in Liminal Situations

The importance of learning to listen, rather than of devising a cunning plan, is highlighted not only by Patrick's story but also in several passages in the Gospels. In Mark 6, for example, the disciples, faced with a major logistical problem, came up with a very logical solution. The thousands gathered to hear Jesus were hungry and the disciples' response was entirely rational: 'Send them away so that they may go into the surrounding country and villages and buy something for themselves to eat'.

If I had been in their shoes, I would have said exactly the same thing. Their initial approach to Jesus reminds me of much of my praying as I often suggest to God how He might or could possibly handle the situations that concern me. Jesus' response was counter-intuitive and defied logic: 'You feed them'. We know the rest of the story. He spoke a blessing over the little they had but despite the unexpected nature of Jesus' directive to them, they had ultimately listened and carried out his instructions.

Paradoxically, this story is encouraging because we can easily be just as dense as the disciples but perhaps God can get through to us also. *The disciples had to learn that successful ministry would be based on hearing and obeying the voice of God.* In a similar vein, Patrick's ministry was founded entirely on his having heard God speak to him, including receiving his call to return to Ireland.

It was following his years of fervent prayer that on one occasion Patrick heard a voice saying, 'Well have you fasted. Very soon you are to travel to your homeland'. The fact that this occurred following six years of intense prayer suggests that God was in no hurry! Perhaps Patrick needed this long experience of exercising faith in adversity to prepare him for his future ministry, as great faith would then be required of him.

History as a whole acts as a real encouragement for those of us in positions of leadership to look to God, rather than finding solutions which rely primarily on our own insights and abilities. Some higher degrees in leadership are essentially an MBA in how to run a large religious organisation. Of course, organisational skills and wisdom are important and rational solutions have their place, such as in Acts 6 when a practical problem desperately needed to be addressed, but liminal situations require something more, a completely different approach in fact.

God's response to the 5th century Church in a liminal situation was to choose Patrick, to form him, and then call him (and, of course, others).[19] Patrick's response was to hear and obey. We too can listen for the voice of the Spirit, seeking to cooperate with Him in whatever difficult circumstances God is using to shape us through and playing whatever part He calls us to play in the destiny of the Church. This is, of course, nowhere near as easy as it sounds, but, though it may take a lifetime to learn, in God's hands it is full of hope for the future.

---

[19] There were many other Christian missionaries who were ministering in Ireland, particularly in the South-east and some, such as Declan of Ardmore, were reputed to have had significant success.

PART 2

LEADERSHIP & CALLING

3

Call

The process by which God prepared Patrick for ministry illustrates the importance of both life experience and the activity of the Holy Spirit in leadership formation. It was primarily through hardship and facing challenges that God transformed Patrick, both in terms of his spiritual formation and in shaping his character:

> I remained on in Ireland, and that not of my own choosing, until I almost perished. However, it was very good for me, since God straightened me out, and he prepared me for what I would be today.[20]

Patrick's story of captivity in Ireland, which prepared him for his future role as the Apostle to the Irish, illustrates how God equips us for the role in life for which he has ordained us. In addition to his having to exercise faith in adversity, Patrick was also prepared for his role by learning the Irish language and, presumably, applying himself to understand something of their culture, including their beliefs and rituals. This involved skills and knowledge acquired through everyday experience which would stand him in good stead in his future role. Leadership today, whether that of leading a church, a homegroup or a ministry, similarly requires the skills and life experiences

---

[20] *Confessio* 28

gained through a wide variety of everyday ordinary activities, such as working with others to earn a living, exercising hospitality (which Paul exhorted his readers in Rome to practise), learning to be tactful or raising a family.[21] Perhaps you can recall formative experiences which have shaped your own life and vocation and through which you have acquired relevant skills and wisdom for ministry.

But over and above the acquisition of skills, perhaps the main preparation for Patrick's future role was the way in which the Holy Spirit worked in and through the circumstances of his life to shape his character and help him acquire a real-life faith. Alongside experiences which were mainly positive, you may also be able to recall difficult circumstances that were either challenging or painful but through which, under God's hand, you acquired practical wisdom for living and learned lessons to better equip you for life. This has resonance with the process used by a sculptor who works repeatedly on a block of marble to reveal the potential that lies within. Real life in all its messiness, heartache and hardship was Patrick's primary place of ministerial formation, his seminary. In such circumstances Patrick's trust in God grew in ways that echo the words of David written centuries earlier:

> The Lord who delivered me from the paw of the lion and from the paw of the bear will deliver me from the hand of the Philistine. (1 Samuel 17:37)

It is God who prepares us and qualifies us as ministers (2 Corinthians 3:6), and this fact seems to be more important and to carry more weight than any formal education, however helpful that may be. Undoubtedly theological education is of great value, but much more fundamental is the faith developed and forged in the trials and tribulation of life.

---

[21] Romans 12:13, 1 Timothy 3:1-5.

Redirection

The second essential factor to be considered in our preparation for ministry is the need for an active and living relationship with the third person of the Trinity. At several key turning points in his life, Patrick had a series of prophetic revelations associated with dreams or visions to guide him in particular directions.

As we saw earlier, after six years of prayer, God indicated to Patrick that his release from captivity was imminent. Subsequently, to that end, Patrick was told by God that a ship had been prepared for him and, in response, he made his way towards the specific port to which God had directed him. Patrick did not know the whereabouts of the port 200 miles away but appears to have been directed by a form of Holy Spirit sat nav to arrive at his destination:

> I had never been to the place, nor did I know anyone there... It was in the strength of God that I went – God who turned the direction of my life to good; I feared nothing while I was on the journey to that ship.[22]

There he found a boat and asked the sailors if he might join them on their voyage. Despite the initial disdain of the crew, they finally called him to join them and agreed to take him across the sea to Britain.[23]

This journey, however, conjures up the phrase 'out of the frying pan and into the fire', for not only was the place where they landed uninhabited, but also they soon ran out of food and found themselves facing starvation. It is not always the case that our obedience to the voice of the Spirit results in an

---

[22] *Confessio* 17

[23] Some scholars think they landed in continental Europe, and Patrick later travelled to his homeland, but according to Patrick's 7th century biographer Muirchu, Britain was where the boat came ashore.

Call

improvement in our situation or positive results in the short-term. The crew challenged Patrick, asking why, if his God was so powerful, were they in this awful situation. He responded that they should trust in God with their whole heart. Amazingly, shortly after this interchange, a herd of pigs wandered across their path and they were able to feast on roast pork! From that time on food was in plentiful supply.

Some years later, Patrick was again captured, becoming a slave for a second time. On this occasion, incredibly, he escaped after two months - the exact period which God had indicated to Patrick that he would remain in captivity - and made his way back to his parents in Britain. He was free at last, but his years in captivity had radically changed and reorientated Patrick.

Once he had returned to his home in Britain, he had a dream, described by Patrick as a 'vision in the night' of an Irishman who visited him and gave him a letter labelled 'the voice of the Irish'.[24] As Patrick read the letter, he heard the voice of the Irish living near the Atlantic shouting to him, 'O holy boy, we beg you to come again and walk among us'. Patrick was overwhelmed as this plea from those in darkness greatly moved him. He described his emotional response as one of being 'broken-hearted'.

Although our way of hearing God may differ substantially from Patrick's experience, a calling from God is nonetheless essential. We commonly refer to having a vocation, the term vocation being derived from the Latin *vocare*, to call. If we lack awareness of having been called, it is unlikely that we will persist in ministry when difficulties arise, or if we are unjustly opposed. It may be the case, as suggested by the stories of some of the biblical prophets, that receiving a clear call is in some way connected to increased likelihood of opposition and

---

[24] *Confessio* 23

to the need to be able to reassure ourselves that we are in the right place.[25] Patrick's dream was pivotal and triggered his return as a missionary to Ireland. His parents though, quite understandably, were set against any course of action that might prove to be dangerous:

> A few years later I was again with my parents in Britain. They welcomed me as a son, and they pleaded with me that, after all the many tribulations I had undergone, I should never leave them again.[26]

The new Patrick was, however, resolute and being open to God, he trained as a priest and eventually was ordained as a bishop. He then began the journey back to the land of his former captivity. This major redirection would have been unlikely to have occurred without God's direct and evocative intervention in Patrick's life at this time.

Discerning a Call

Every call is unique, whether it is primarily to serve our family and church, be involved with others in our place of work or community, go overseas or undertake church leadership in some form. But this leaves us with the question as to how we discern our call. Popular today are gift analysis questionnaires based on the lists of gifts in passages such as 1 Corinthians 12 and Romans 12. While these lists are not exhaustive, they can help us explore our unique blend of gifts, whether 'spiritual' or 'natural' (although I am not convinced the Bible makes this distinction as everything is from God).

Another approach, often employed in the training of church

---

[25] This link between call and opposition or hardship is seen clearly in the case of Isaiah and Jeremiah (Isaiah 6:9-13; Jeremiah 1:8).

[26] *Confessio* 23

leaders in settings such as seminaries, is to use one of the personality tools available, such as the Myers-Briggs Type Indicator (MBTI). Again, this can be helpful in our coming to appreciate where we are likely to find a good fit between our personality and our role in the Church. It is likely, for example, that extraverts are more suited to evangelism than extreme introverts, who might find that too much people-contact is exhausting rather than energising.

Yet I am less than convinced that these methods actually help us discern our call. There is a problem with putting too much weight on these sorts of tools and the problem is the Bible! God's call to a particular ministry can actually be at odds with the conclusions drawn from gift or personality analysis, however useful they may be in developing self-understanding. Imagine for one moment that Moses, Jeremiah, and Isaiah had attended a course entitled 'discerning your gift'. Moses would never have ticked any of the boxes relating to spoken ministry and his self-assessment would have stated 'I am slow of speech' (Exodus 4:10). So convinced was he that God's call was a bad fit with his gifts that he pleaded, 'Please send someone else' (4:13).

Jeremiah considered himself wholly unsuited to be a prophet because of his lack of experience and the fact that others would not take him seriously, pleading, 'I am only a youth'. God's response failed entirely to take Jeremiah's own gift analysis into consideration (Jeremiah 1:6). Similarly, Isaiah excluded himself from a spoken ministry because he felt he was not separate enough from the surrounding cultural malaise: 'I am a man of unclean lips and I dwell in the midst of a people of unclean lips' (Isaiah 6:5). Yet, despite the fact that in their own eyes they evidently lacked the required gifts or dispositions, these biblical characters were nonetheless called to exercise a spoken ministry. It is, I suggest, more important to hear the voice of the Spirit than to decide for ourselves what our ministry might be. God's power is, after all, made perfect in weakness and simply relying on our strengths may be unhelpful in this process of discernment (2 Corinthians 12:9).

Hearing God

> And the Lord came and stood, calling as at other times, 'Samuel! Samuel!' and Samuel said, 'Speak, Lord, for your servant hears'. (1 Samuel 3:10)

The process of discerning our call involves learning to recognise how God habitually communicates with us. We have seen that, in Patrick's case, this was primarily through dreams and visions.[27] I have had one dream that I would consider to have been God guiding the direction of my ministry, but dreams are not the usual way in which I hear God. I have learned that when God seeks to communicate something major to me it most often comes as an inner conviction which grows and becomes stronger. This is difficult to describe but it is different from having reached a conclusion or come to an opinion on something. In fact, it is more a case of 'where did that come from?' and it doesn't go away or fade with time.

In the 1980s, I had an enduring conviction that I should study because there would be a time when I needed it and wouldn't have time to do it. This growing conviction fitted with an earlier prophecy that I would be a teacher in the Church, but otherwise it seemed rather strange. It felt as if it was from left field, since I had already read widely in the areas of theology, church history, psychology etc, and my knowledge base seemed adequate for my role in teaching and church leadership. But I took this conviction seriously and, in

---

[27] There is a need to exercise caution in relying on guidance through prophecy or dreams and test it carefully. Some people are 'visual thinkers' and can easily assume that their imaginative thoughts are from God.

response, I allocated a certain percentage of my income to purchase relevant books, read more and eventually pursued a higher degree in theology.

I went on to teach more formally in different settings, but somehow none of this quite seemed to fulfil what I had sensed earlier about the time that was coming. At several points I questioned whether my instinct had been correct as I didn't seem to need to draw on much of the study I had undertaken. In fact, it wasn't until more than 30 years after my original conviction that what I had seemed to discern proved actually to be the case. In more recent years there has been dialogue with the Vatican, conference speaking and writing – none of which would have been possible without the preparation I undertook in earlier years.

God may well speak to each of us in different ways, such as highlighting a passage of Scripture to us, through the words of others or, like Patrick, through a dream - but whatever form this takes, our first task is learning to discern whether and when God is speaking to us. Only with discernment will we clearly hear His call and it may be useful at this point to give some time to reviewing the ways in which God has spoken to you about your present or future leadership role. Patrick's story highlights the importance of an awareness of the specificity of our call, its shape and the particular contours that make it unique. Of course, we then need to respond to that call and this may involve a change of location or geography (as with Patrick), developing certain gifts, focusing on specific areas of service and, always and inevitably, sacrifice. These are all aspects of our call to ministry that are explored further in this book.

4

Conflict

Patrick obeyed the heavenly vision and returned to Ireland sometime around 432 AD. The 'mythical Patrick', as described by Muirchu, did this in a swashbuckling manner, exhibiting great courage and showing no fear in confronting either the High King or more minor kings and druids. In reality, however, obeying the call to return to the Irish was to embrace a life of insecurity and uncertainty in the face of considerable risk and threat. Patrick 'put up with insults from unbelievers', endured 'many persecutions even involving chains', recounting that there were, in fact, 'twelve dangers that threatened [his] life'.[28]

His life was so marked by these features that some of his contemporaries questioned his actions: 'Why does this man put himself in danger among hostile people who do not know God?'[29] Patrick reported that such criticism was not motivated by malice. His fellow clergy simply could not understand why he was prepared to take such a risky path in life, even venturing into a land of barbarians with no guarantee for his safety whatsoever. But Patrick had received a call to return to Ireland which superseded these and other such concerns. It is sometimes the case for us too that our contemporaries are not able to comprehend the nature of our call. This might

---

[28] *Confessio* 35 & 37

[29] *Confessio* 46

particularly be so if, as with Patrick, we are perceived as taking a path less well-trodden or of making choices that limit other possibilities for ministry.

As we have seen, Patrick's call was set against the backdrop of his family pressuring him to remain in the relative security of western Britain. Retracing his steps back to Ireland seemed wholly unwise, given his previous captivity, and the reaction of Patrick's parents, having lost their son as a teenager, was perfectly understandable. Not only were they painfully aware of the risks involved, but they were also, by the standard of their day, heading toward old age and may have wanted him to remain at home for that reason. Patrick, however, was required to put aside his parents' concerns; he also had to disregard any concern *he* might have had for his own safety.

Holy Indifference

In this conflict of interests, he exhibited what has been described as 'holy indifference' towards both his own and his parents' wishes. This term, coined by St. Ignatius of Loyola in the 16th century, does not mean that we do not care or are indifferent to ourselves or to others. Rather, it has to do with cultivating spiritual freedom - an interior freedom of the mind and heart which allows us to make choices, whatever the circumstances, keeping God's call at the centre of our lives.[30] Without this spiritual freedom, we become excessively attached to particular people, places, possessions, acclaim, or titles which can, under certain circumstances, hinder us from doing God's will. Many of these things are good in themselves when ordered and directed by the love of God. They become

---

[30] Kevin O'Brien, *The Ignatian Adventure*. Chicago, Loyola Press, 2011, p.57.

'disordered attachments' when they push God out of the centre of our lives and become the key to our identity.[31] Having spiritual freedom (holy indifference) allows us to do God's will even when this is challenging or requires considerable sacrifice on our part. We can usefully reflect on the degree to which our own choices are – or have been - governed by external factors or internal drives that, while not sinful in themselves, may distract us from God's call on our life. In addition, we may have further thoughts as to what might help us develop a greater degree of holy indifference.

So, Patrick's 'indifference' wasn't due to recklessness or adventure-seeking but was related to his having a higher call on his life. The vision mentioned in the previous chapter had gripped him and he felt impelled to return to the land of his captivity. But this time there was a crucial difference; not only was he free from his captors, but he was also spiritually free to serve the God who had called him.

Looking back on his ministry, Patrick recorded in his *Confession* that he had baptised thousands and many noble Irish men and women had become monks and nuns. This had only been achieved by having freely embraced much personal risk, as well as by his having laid aside the attachments of home and kin which could so easily have prevented him from responding to God's call. This was particularly the case at the outset of his ministry when, the development of his trust in God apart, there had been no guarantee of success.

Opposition in Ireland

The Ireland to which Patrick freely returned was a feudal society, consisting of rural clan-like tribes, probably about 150 in all. These were grouped into regional kingdoms which were

---

[31] See O'Brien (2011), p.58.

under the overall leadership of the High King of Ireland. To make headway with the task before him Patrick would first need to convert the local kings to gain access to those further down the social hierarchy.[32] He embarked on this mission to a very socially stratified society with little in the way of recognised position or status. Security depended on being personally connected to the various clans and Patrick was definitely an outsider in that respect. As Michael Haykin writes:

> Although Patrick had status in Roman Britain as the son of a decurion [council member], in Ireland he has no standing at all, for he was a stranger without relatives, and hence without a network of safety and influence.[33]

The situation concerning Patrick's status in Ireland is perhaps more complex than this might imply, as it was incumbent on kings to show hospitality to strangers and to ensure that they were fed.[34] Patrick was an educated visitor and some kings may have respected the cultural requirement to be generous to such persons, but clearly not all did. He recounted the ongoing hardships he had endured as part of his mission: 'for not a day passes but I expect to be killed or waylaid or taken into slavery or assaulted in some other way'.

Alongside presenting kings with the claims of Christianity, Patrick would have faced opposition from druids, the priests of Celtic religion who officiated at ceremonies. These were aristocratic men who had studied long and hard to acquire

---

[32] Kings were figureheads rather than lawmakers and would lead their tribe in times of war. See Anne Hughes, *The Celtic Church: Origins, Developments and Themes*. Newtownards, Colourprint Educational, 2018, p.9-10.

[33] This obligation was embedded in law. Michael Haykin, *Patrick of Ireland: His Life and Impact*. Fern, Ross-shire, Christian Focus, 2014, p.63.

[34] Peter Beresford Ellis, *A Brief History of the Celts*. London, Robinson, 2003, p.176

wisdom and to learn how to foretell the future. They also communicated moral values to those in power and acted as their trusted advisors. Although Patrick does not specifically describe opposition from druids, this would have been likely since his very existence as well as his message challenged their privileged place in Irish society as the guardians of wisdom, and the arrival of Christianity meant that eventually they were displaced from this powerful position.

Opposition in Britain

> For it is not an enemy who taunts me - then I could bear it... But it is you, a man, my equal, my companion, my familiar friend. (Psalm 55:12-13)

It was not only in the land of his calling in which Patrick faced opposition, since many in Britain also opposed his ministry to those they considered beyond the pale of the civilised Romano-British world. After all, in their version of God's dealing with humankind, the Roman Empire had been the chosen vehicle for transmitting the gospel. Patrick suffered considerably from the effects of gossip and slander, and many of his contemporaries tried to prevent his mission to the uncouth, uncivilised enemies of the Romano-British.

Much of Patrick's autobiography is a defence of his ministry against the backdrop of the accusations of others. The source of his most sustained and painful opposition was a previously close Christian friend, rather than the pagan rulers of Ireland. The basis of this hurtful attack was an accusation discrediting Patrick. Its exact nature is unclear, but it was based on Patrick's confession to this former friend of an unnamed sin committed in his early days before being taken to Ireland as a slave. This person had initially supported and encouraged Patrick to pursue his ministry to the Irish but had subsequently decided to make Patrick's past misdemeanour public.

Anecdotally, this dynamic does not seem to be uncommon. Previously supportive friends and colleagues can eventually come to oppose us (and we should note that another dynamic can also occur - confronting those to whom we are close can also result in their seeking to discredit us). These are regrettable and deeply painful scenarios, but they need not surprise us if we appreciate the stories of those like Patrick who had to press on despite such opposition.

The motivation for this attempt to discredit Patrick is uncertain and we can only guess what Patrick's sin had been. His defence was simply to state that God had adequately disciplined and changed him during his captivity. At this difficult and testing time, Patrick had a further experience of God speaking to him in a vision one night: 'He who touches you as it were touches the pupil of my eye'.[35] Understandably, this released in Patrick a newfound boldness and confidence.[36]

In addition to this injurious charge, rumours attacking his integrity were also being spread far and wide. Patrick had accrued wealth from generous donors and he had used this to pay kings to secure his safe passage through their territories, as well as to purchase the freedom of Christian slaves. False accusations were spread, claiming that his ministry was motivated by financial gain. Patrick countered this by reporting that he had 'sold [his] noble rank', implying that he had taken the wealth inherited from his parents and used it to fund his mission out of his own pocket. To remain above suspicion, he had even returned gifts which devoted women had laid on the altar. There are circumstances in which those in leadership

---

[35] *Confessio* 29

[36] Dr Martin Luther King Jr recounted a similar experience when he was receiving up to thirty threatening phone calls a day. He heard the voice of God telling him to stand up for righteousness and assuring him of His presence. Following this, he engaged with his life's work with renewed courage.

need to have been seen to have acted with integrity, even if this involves loss of income or other benefits, and this was one such example.

Patrick was forced to defend himself and he did so by employing arguments like those used in the second letter to the Corinthians, in which Paul highlights his suffering as being a mark of genuine apostleship. Like Paul, Patrick recounted that he had undergone 'tribulations, many setbacks, captivity' and had endured many persecutions as well as having resisted frequent temptations. There are striking similarities between Patrick's description of his suffering and Paul's list of trials in 2 Corinthians 11:21-23 and Patrick most probably wanted his readers to be aware of the parallels. It is also clear to both Paul and Patrick that the fact that God would one day hold them personally to account was of much more importance than any human judgement in this present age might be.

Conflict Comes with the Territory

Leadership inevitably involves a degree of conflict and, at times, there might also be a need to confront others. This is not altogether unsurprising and, to a certain extent, is to be expected. It does not necessarily signal failure on our part. We are called to be peacemakers, but this does not mean that we should seek to keep the peace at any cost. My observation is that those new to church leadership often set out with the belief that if they simply love everyone, they will never need to confront people or address situations when things have gone awry. It is true that, along with a desire for God to be honoured, love has to be our primary motivation, and love does cover a multitude of sins, but we are enjoined to address serious issues in the life of the Church and to do so with clarity. Sometimes it is simply the case that people are mistaken or unwise in their speech or actions; at other times we are dealing with the realities of pride, politicking to get people on our side, gossip or other such things, which, if left unaddressed, will most certainly cause harm, hurt and division in a church.

Sometimes conflict involves an attack on those in ministry. As we have seen, one form of opposition for Patrick involved rumourmongering concerning the handling of finance. I was, in fact, recently with a church leader who had similarly suffered false accusations of financial impropriety being spread about him. This was motivated by malice and, as a result, the mental health of the leader in question deteriorated considerably. Christians (including those in leadership) are, sadly, not immune from the temptation to gossip. Another friend was falsely defamed with the intent to draw people away from his church and to facilitate the start of a new church under different leadership. I suspect the slander involved may have been a result of defensive behaviour from someone with narcissistic personality traits who felt the need to prove himself.

At times, there is a clear need to call leaders themselves to account when their behaviour towards others is questionable and Paul's confrontation with Peter is a case in point (Galatians 2:11-14). This sort of overt calling to account frequently occurs late in the game once complaints are numerous and can no longer be ignored. Perhaps one root cause of our overlooking major faults is that we sometimes value gift above character and are prone to engage in a form of hero worship, believing that our hero can do no wrong. Sometimes the Scripture 'touch not the Lord's anointed and do my prophets no harm' is misapplied to justify this form of laissez-faire attitude (Psalm 105:15; 1 Chronicles 16:22). In fact, 'the Lord's anointed' refers to the whole people of Israel, rather than to an individual, and as such it was a warning given to the surrounding nations.

Another reason we may be reluctant to address issues with another person, especially with another leader, is that the actual process of doing so is difficult. Confronting others is particularly difficult if a major element in our motivation for ministry is the need to be liked. It requires courage to initiate and, even once initiated, the process may be unfruitful, especially if the person in question either ignores or refuses to consider the issues raised. But we need to decide when a situation requires forbearance (putting up with) and when confrontation is needed.

Only sociopaths enjoy confronting others - most of us are anxious in situations where there is conflict, and this is healthy, a sign that we do not wish to offend people or make things unpleasant. When challenge is required, we should remember that to do this skilfully is something we learn from experience. Many, including church leaders, tend to shy away from conflict resolution and still others lack the skill and experience to know how best to approach conflict. Conflict is all too often too hot to handle and too difficult to resolve but some people can do it in such a way that it is not offensive or overly awkward. Possibly the most skilful approach is to be able to ask the sorts of questions that help others challenge themselves.

Resolving Differences

The inability to resolve differences is a major reason why churches split and many of us, if not most of us, will have had the experience of there being unresolved conflict. The term 'conflict' is broad, covering everything from overt hostility, as in the case of Patrick's opponents, to simply having different views on an issue. While conflict driven by pride or ambition is likely to be destructive, if it is simply disagreement arising out of differences of perspective it actually has the potential for us to work things through to a good solution.

During my time as the programme leader for a Masters Degree in Missional Leadership, I gained the impression, based on student feedback, that the most impactful unit of the whole course was that on resolving conflict. The study material brought the root cause of most situations of conflict into focus, pointing out that we often simply see things differently because of our circumstances, life experiences or personality. The main thing I gleaned from reviewing the literature on conflict resolution is the need to listen and communicate that we understand another's point of view *before* we explain our own.

This can have a positive outcome as listening attentively and seeking to resolve differing views allows us to consider more factors than if we were to simply rely on our own limited perspective (which is why one-person leadership usually ends badly). As someone once put it, 'a point of view is just a view from a particular point' and the creative potential in seeking to resolve differences is easily overlooked. For example, one person will view a suggested course of action with a focus on how it will affect people, while another will focus on the likelihood of its effectiveness in reaching a goal, so hearing one another can enable us to make decisions based on a much fuller appreciation of the issues. This sort of difference of perspective seems to have been the root cause of the Paul-Barnabas split outlined in Act 15:36-41. Some of the literature on addressing conflict seems to me to be hopelessly optimistic! Resolution is sadly not always possible even where there is the desire to follow God - Paul and Barnabas decided to go their separate ways having failed to agree.

Direct Confrontation

When a more collaborative resolution process is not possible, direct confrontation may be necessary. We see this in Patrick's *Letter to the Soldiers of Coroticus* since severe warnings were needed to address their appalling behaviour in killing Irish Christians and abducting others as slaves. Paul, as mentioned, adopted this direct approach in his second letter to the Corinthians, where he pulled no punches but told it straight. This is uncomfortable but necessary to ensure that the work of God is not derailed and that it bears good fruit.

In the majority of cases, confrontation needs to be less forceful than in the shocking case of Coroticus' pirates, where stern warnings were clearly necessary. In most instances, it should be approached prayerfully, humbly, and certainly not defensively. We need to be self-aware and own any issues raised that we ourselves may have. We should also be aware that leadership confers some authority in the minds of church members, and this requires a sensitive and gentle approach so that people don't feel accused or condemned. It is, however, usually best to be straightforward and clear as the message is unlikely to get across if we are too 'tactful' and avoid addressing our concerns. Having said that, there is always the possibility that we have got hold of the wrong end of the stick and listening to the other is crucial. The end point is 'to win a brother' not to prove a point (Matthew 18:15-20).

We also should bear in mind that according to several passages in Scripture, confrontation and mutual instruction are the responsibility, not just of leaders but of the whole Church, as we seek to enable one another to be conformed to the image of Christ (James 5:19-20, Romans 15:14). We, the Church, are to teach and admonish *one another* rather than take every conflict to an overburdened leadership group (Colossians 3:16). Yet many in our congregations feel ill-prepared for this task, so it is a case not just of teaching but also of modelling biblical ways to approach conflict resolution so that people in our churches become equipped to 'teach and admonish one another'. As we see in the case of Patrick, if leadership is to be effective it simply is not possible if areas causing conflict are constantly avoided and never addressed.

PART 3

COURAGE TO LEAD

5

Confidence

> My name is Patrick. I am a sinner, a simple country person, and the least of all believers. I am looked down upon by many.[37]

The last chapter explored the *external* conflict that Patrick faced in Ireland, as well as the opposition he experienced from colleagues and even from a former friend. In this chapter we turn to the topic of his *inner* turmoil and conflicts, particularly those related to the feelings of inadequacy or self-doubt which so often accompany God's call to individuals, and which can actually be even more debilitating than the criticism and attack of others. Patrick's feelings of inadequacy focused particularly on what he felt to be a lack of proper education.

In fact, as a member of the upper echelon of Romano-British society, Patrick received what would have been regarded as a good education, involving as it did, learning to speak and write Latin. Patrick was, however, acutely aware of the fact that he wrote in the older Latin of the Bible, rather than in the more sophisticated version learned by more advanced scholars. He appears to have been embarrassed by the fact that he had 'not been a student like other men' who 'drank in equally well both the law and the sacred writings, and never had to change their

---

[37] *Confessio* 1

way of speaking since childhood, but always grew better and better at it'.[38] He felt his lack of scholarship keenly and at one point described himself as being 'inexperienced in all things'.[39]

Patrick regarded himself as a rustic nobody, 'imperfect in many things', and he lamented the fact that his learning was interrupted by his captivity as a teenager. He was certain that his readers would easily spot his 'lack of expertise and polish'. Today, we might say that he suffered from Imposter Syndrome! He was in good company since, as previously noted, Isaiah, Jeremiah and Moses similarly felt that, lacking the necessary maturity and/or skills, they were unsuited to God's call.[40] There is, therefore, hope for us all!

With the benefit of hindsight, Patrick came to realise that despite regarding himself as being poorly prepared educationally, God had used him to great effect. In actual fact, our experience of God and his ways over many years is not to be underestimated, as we can learn to draw upon it in our feelings of inadequacy. If we find ourselves able to put aside our internal struggles, we may often achieve a measure of success through our obedience to God's call. Self-doubt may well inhibit us, but experience often demonstrates that God can and does use us even when we have little confidence in our abilities. It is often the case that while those who are competent lack confidence, those who appear most self-confident sometimes actually turn out to be least competent.

Despite these internal restraints, Patrick eventually nonetheless became a bishop before returning to Ireland. This process required a certain amount of learning, although probably the training was delivered mainly through an

---

[38] *Confessio* 9

[39] *Confessio* 49

[40] See Isaiah 6:5, Jeremiah 1:6, and Exodus 3:11.

apprenticeship system during which Patrick would have assisted an existing bishop in his duties. It is unlikely that he studied for a prolonged period even though Muirchu has Patrick spending several years under tuition in Gaul.[41] Muirchu suggests that Patrick realised his need to supplement his experiential learning with a different sort of preparation which involved understanding the 'divine wisdom'. He reports that Patrick set out on a journey to Rome to study there but was side-tracked when he met bishop Germanus of Auxerre in France, under whom, according to Muirchu, he studied for a long time. Although Muirchu's account is most probably inaccurate some support can be found in Patrick's writing for at least a short visit to Gaul. In old age he expressed an affection for his 'brethren' in Gaul and a desire to go there to see his old friends.

Scholars are divided in their opinions as to whether Patrick did spend much time training in Gaul but, on balance, this seems unlikely given his rudimentary Latin. It is more likely that he trained mainly in Britain. His writing demonstrates an in-depth knowledge of the Bible and of the theology of the Trinity, but little else that would indicate 'book learning' or the training in rhetoric which was deemed the mark of a well-educated person, and which, in Gaul, would have formed part of an esteemed education.

Despite a lack of trust in his own abilities, Patrick's confidence in God had increased considerably during the hardship he suffered as a slave, herding pigs and sheep, and particularly as he learned the value of fervent prayer. As a result of prayer, Patrick experienced God as his guide and rescuer, making the preparation for his future role primarily experiential. In addition, he came to understand the significance of the events of his life through the lens of

---

[41] Muirchu's *Life of Patrick* 5

Scripture. This combination of experience plus reflection on that experience through the framework of the Bible provided Patrick with the deep roots in God he would need for his ministry. An experiential knowledge of God as our guide and deliverer not only enables us to have confidence for our own future but is also the basis on which we can communicate such confidence to others (2 Corinthians 1:5-6). In keeping with Patrick's example, have you been able to process your own experiences by viewing them through the lens of Scripture?

Patrick's Personality

Before we delve deeper into Patrick's story it is worth considering alternative explanations for his apparent overly modest appraisal of himself. One possibility is that Patrick's comments were merely a reflection of his great humility rather than the result of markedly sober introspection. Another explanation for his self-effacing statements is that his protestations of innocence were a smokescreen for the fact that he was guilty as accused. In the latter case, he would have been writing in a rather manipulative way to appeal to a wider audience and to get them on his side against his detractors. Perhaps naively, I am inclined to take him more at face value and regard Patrick's *Confession* as a genuine expression of his innermost thoughts.

I do, however, think that some consideration of his personality is worthwhile, as his assessment of his abilities does seem to be unduly negative. For one thing, as Thomas O'Loughlin notes, Patrick was well educated compared to most people in his day and was bi- or even tri-lingual, since in addition to Latin, as already mentioned, he must have learned Irish and at home probably spoke British (which resembled Welsh). Assessing his skill in Latin is also difficult, as he was someone who wrote only occasionally rather than as a professional writer. He was certainly able to handle biblical texts with great skill and effectiveness, so his academic skills were far from rudimentary.[42] He exhibited critical thinking and could mount a powerful argument.

While perhaps it is not possible to draw clear conclusions about Patrick's personality, some interesting observations emerge when we think in terms of modern psychology. Psychologists suggest that personality profiling tests all measure the same five basic traits. These spell OCEAN and are Openness to experience; Conscientiousness; Extraversion; Agreeableness; and Neuroticism. These terms are not used with any sense of moral judgment, they simply represent the spectrum of human personality types, and an OCEAN test will score us for each of these traits relative to those of the general population.

Patrick's writings betray a degree of vulnerability and that he was clearly sensitive to external criticism which added to his inner sense of being ill-equipped. These features are reminiscent of the trait 'neuroticism', which involves a tendency to worry, feel pessimistic and insecure and this may suggest that, like me, Patrick might have scored above average for this particular trait.[43] If this is indeed the case, it would have made his achievements even more remarkable, as his battle was not just external but also internal, having to fight against such feelings.

Such dynamics are not uncommon. Even today, I received a message from someone with a long track record of successful ministry requesting prayer for an event he is running very soon. His feelings of inadequacy, perhaps even

---

[42] See Thomas O'Loughlin, *Saint Patrick: The Man and his Work*. London, SPCK, 1999, p.26-28.

[43] https://www.forbes.com/sites/tomaspremuzic/2022/06/07/are-successful-people-more-neurotic/# accessed 08.01.23

of being overwhelmed, fail to reflect past performance. It is estimated that nearly a third of people, including a proportion of prominent high achievers, score well above average for neuroticism. Stories like that of Patrick can reassure us as leaders facing this issue, that a lack of self-confidence does not disqualify us and that it is possible to not just survive but thrive in our calling even when our internal dialogue, our 'inner critic', mitigates against this.

Patrick's Confidence

In addition to his internal battle, in returning to Ireland, Patrick was sent to a place which, in those days, would have been deemed an evangelist's graveyard with few stories of success to bolster his confidence in his mission. This makes his return an act of pure faith in God, trusting in His ability to act in and through him.

It seems evident that Patrick's confidence was not based on skills acquired through experience, innate self-confidence, learning, or his natural abilities; it was based wholly on the fact that God was at work in the world and that He had already shaped Patrick's character, particularly during his time of enslavement, so that he could be used. In particular, he had learned to trust in Someone bigger than himself. Indeed, an alternative title that has been suggested for Patrick's *Confession* is '*Patrick's Declaration of the Great Works of God*'. Oliver Davies, an expert on Celtic manuscripts suggests that this is indeed a fitting title, in keeping with Patrick's intention.[44]

At least three separate strands can be traced to Patrick's confidence: his trust in the Holy Spirit as an active agent in his life, his rootedness in Scripture, and his authority as a bishop.

---

[44] Oliver Davies, *Celtic Spirituality*. New York, Paulist Press, 1999, p.28.

We'll look at the first two elements, the Holy Spirit and Scripture, in this chapter and focus on his office as a bishop in the next.

The Holy Spirit

This section could be titled 'Prayer and the Holy Spirit' for the two topics seem inseparable in Patrick's experience. Thomas O'Loughlin sees his years in slavery as a form of probation with an initiation into the life of the Spirit, with his leaving of Ireland to return to Britain as an equivalent to graduation.[45] Patrick had gained what was necessary for his future, having learned to trust God and to rely on the Holy Spirit's leading. His story acts as a reminder that the same dynamic, trust in God, needs to be the foundation for our own ministry. It also highlights the way in which faith is formed within us through our facing challenges with a prayerful attitude.

A reliance on the Spirit is evident in Patrick's accounts of the experiences where God communicated to him through a vision or a voice. It was in response to hundreds of daily prayers that the Spirit directed his escape from slavery and he attributed his devotion to prayer to the unseen inner workings of the Holy Spirit within: 'I was up before dawn to pray... I now understand this: at that time the Spirit was fervent within me'.

Shortly after crossing the Irish Sea, whilst travelling through the 'desert' with his companions from the ship, he experienced a physical attack from Satan in the form of the sensation of a heavy weight crushing him. He called out to the Sun, and it rose, dispelling the darkness. Again, he attributed this prayer for deliverance to the action of the Spirit crying out through him.[46]

---

[45] O'Loughlin (1999), p.41.

[46] *Confessio* 20. Scholars debate why he might call out to the Sun – was it a

Confidence

The final revelation he recorded, in the context of the criticism from his colleagues in the British Church, was the dream in which it was revealed to him that those who opposed Patrick opposed God himself. He might have been finished psychologically and spiritually by this experience of opposition, but instead he drew immense strength from this encounter with the Spirit.[47]

Despite his sense of loneliness, which was evident when he wrote of desiring to visit family in Britain and friends in Gaul, he records that he was 'bound in the Spirit, who assures me that if I were to do this, I would be held guilty'.[48] In his *Letter to the Soldiers of Coroticus*, he similarly stated that he was not free to visit his relatives, again due to the inner witness of the Spirit.[49] The ministry of the Holy Spirit in his life countered his sense of inadequacy, he knew that his life and ministry had been shaped by the Spirit and he had a strong inner sense that he was in the right place at the right time.

The Word

Patrick has been described as 'a man of one book' and he had a clear grasp of doctrine and its practical implications. As Michael Haykin rightly points out, it would be anachronistic to describe Patrick as an Evangelical, particularly as he was devoted to monasticism, but, just like Evangelicals today, he regarded the Bible as the only book that really mattered.[50]

---

symbol of the Risen Christ? He certainly attributed his deliverance to Christ's intervention. Another possibility is that he was calling not to Helias (the Sun) but to Elijah. Or, it may have been that because of the physically oppressive, extreme darkness of the experience, it was only natural to call out to the Sun.

[47] *Confessio* 29 & 30

[48] *Confessio* 43

[49] *Letter to the Soldiers of Coroticus* 10

[50] Michael Haykin, *Patrick of Ireland: His Life and Impact*. Fern, Ros-shire,

Scripture certainly shaped the way in which he regarded his ministry. For instance, he believed that taking the gospel to Ireland, the very edge of the then-known world, would be a fulfilment of the words of Jesus which indicated that once the furthermost parts of the earth had been reached, the end would come (Matthew 24:14).

For Patrick, the Bible was much, much more than a wonderful book outlining the workings of God in the world. As we read Patrick's writing, it is evident that the Bible was also a very *personal* book for him. Patrick understood the events and shape of his life through a deep engagement with Scripture and the larger contours of the biblical narrative had become the framework in which he existed. The story of the Bible had become so interwoven with his own story that the two were almost synonymous, and he understood his preparation and call to ministry within the overarching narrative provided by Scripture. God's story had become Patrick's story.

I think it is worth reflecting on this process of seeing ourselves as participants in this bigger story. An interesting exercise is to consider which biblical character most captures our imagination as this, assuming that God is involved in our inner world and has a hand in shaping our interests and our desires, can point to the part we are to play in this larger narrative of Scripture.

Yet Scripture provided even more than this as it supplied the actual language for his *Confession* and *Letter*. Scriptural phrases acted as a template for many of the biographical sections in his writing and became the vehicle for Patrick to describe more clearly the activity of God in his life. In writing

---

Christian Focus, 2014, p.98. O'Loughlin (1999), p.50 notes that some scholars have found echoes of Sts. Cyprian and Augustine in Patrick's writing. Nonetheless, Patrick's allusions to Scripture are frequent and Haykin's description seems warranted even if Patrick occasionally draws on other sources.

his *Confession* and the *Letter to the Soldiers of Coroticus* Patrick either quoted directly or adapted phrases from more than 40 verses from Paul's Letter to the Romans alone. In one sentence, for example, he combined such concepts as 'being fellow heirs with Christ,' 'conformed to his image,' and the idea that 'for him and through him and in him' we shall reign (Romans 8:17, 8:29 and 11:36). In fact, this sentence in *Confessio* 59 also alludes to at least 3 other scriptural verses!

The only two books in the New Testament that he didn't directly use or allude to are Philemon and 2 John. His knowledge of the Bible was encyclopaedic, and he was thoroughly immersed in its pages. Being soaked in Scripture is likely to be a prerequisite for effective ministry. This has implications for us too and it also underlines the importance of helping others to similarly immerse themselves in the Bible.

The Word & the Spirit

Patrick's life illustrates that the dynamic of Word and Spirit operating together is powerful and underlines its relevance to leadership today. I write this at a time when some more Conservative Evangelicals may be reluctant to entertain thoughts that at times God can speak to us directly through the Spirit without using Scripture itself, while some more Charismatically inclined Christians may fail to adequately engage with Scripture at depth. Patrick clearly embraced both elements and it is unlikely that his ministry would have been effective or even possible without this synergy.

Patrick's story also has implications for the role of the Bible in the formation of disciples equipped for Christian ministry. In particular, it is worth considering the place that personal engagement with Scripture does or should play in ministry formation. In some circles, great emphasis is placed on academic learning, yet Patrick's more personal engagement with Scripture – his immersion in its pages - seemed to have a greater impact on his life and ministry.

I have greatly benefitted from academic learning and my time at theological college was the best educational experience I have had, but I am also aware that in the course of my own leadership development the most influential leaders (one of whom helped found one of the few British megachurches), though widely read and experienced, had no formal theological qualifications. They learned the skills and function of leadership on the job. What they did have was a depth of engagement with the Spirit and Scripture similar to that highlighted by Patrick's story. Perhaps we should remember that few of the prominent leaders in the New Testament had received rigorous academic training - perhaps only Paul and possibly Apollos.

I hope it is evident that I am not in any way anti-intellectual. I believe that for some leaders, myself included, an academic grounding has been entirely necessary for effectiveness in a specific type of ministry, but perhaps we need to be more discriminating in discerning what kind of preparation is appropriate for certain individuals in particular specific roles. Whatever our thoughts on this topic, and some may feel my views tend towards one extreme, the main point is that confidence comes from our having experience of God the Holy Spirit acting in our lives; experience framed by a personal engagement with Scripture.

6

Commission

> Patrick, a sinner and one truly unlearned.
> I declare myself to be a bishop set up by God in Ireland.[51]

In the previous chapter we saw that Patrick's confidence in his innate abilities was low, but that the impact of the Spirit and the Word in his life engendered great boldness in ministry. A further factor contributing to his confidence was that he was certain that he had been appointed *by God* to the office of a bishop. His opening statement in his *Letter to the Soldiers of Coroticus*, quoted above, demonstrates the importance he placed on this role as an authoritative representative of Jesus Christ. 'I declare myself a bishop' was a way of saying 'take note and listen' and in these words we feel the full weight of the Lord himself behind Patrick. Elsewhere, he quotes the words of Christ to Peter, 'Whatever you bind on earth shall be bound in heaven,' and applies them to all priests who preach the gospel.[52] Patrick clearly placed great value on the significance of ordination and of his own appointment to high office in the Church. That is not to suggest, however, that he viewed his authority as residing in him personally, as

---

[51] *Letter to the Soldiers of Coroticus* 1
[52] *Letter* 6

somehow separate from an active relationship with, and obedience to, God. His role as an authorised representative of the Lord depended entirely on his faithfully communicating the gospel, including those elements some might be tempted to omit, such as the certainty of judgement for those who, like the soldiers of Coroticus, totally ignored the moral implications of faith. His authority was not dependent on his own thoughts and feelings but on the faithful proclamation of the Scriptures: 'These are not my words', Patrick states at one point, 'but words that never lie: those of God and his holy apostles and prophets'.[53]

Patrick's confidence in his ordination as a bishop may present a problem for those of us who, like me, come from church traditions which downplay distinctions made between those who are in leadership and those whom in many circles are referred to as 'laity'. Furthermore, there are those who are averse to any hint of an episcopal system which depends on what is understood as 'apostolic succession' to legitimise ministers. However, most would argue that the recognition of the wider Church as a whole is necessary in confirming someone's call to leadership and most churches have some system of official recognition in place. By way of analogy, I can recall qualifying as a medical doctor and, although still having much to learn, it was reassuring to know that in the eyes of my peers and others, I had completed a process of professional formation and was deemed to be ready for the role, as signified by my new title. Patrick's evident confidence arising from having been ordained might lead us to reflect on the ways in which our own leadership role has been recognised, accepted and confirmed by others – and whether we too draw some degree of confidence from this.

We should note, however, that Patrick did not wear his office

---

[53] *Letter* 20

as a badge of honour. He was still the 'least of all Christians' and an unworthy servant. His role was also one that required perseverance and could be arduous. It was both a privilege and, at the same time, an unglamorous and 'toilsome office of bishop' to which he had been called.[54] Patrick's emphasis on his authority has to be set in the context of his evident humility and his somewhat negative assessment of his innate worth. God was certainly working through Patrick, but there is no hint that Patrick claimed to be the source of these great acts of God.[55] On the contrary, unlike those who might become proud once they have the recognition of others, Patrick remained humble and was surprised that God had deigned to use him.

The Contours of Patrick's Mission

Patrick was not, in fact, the first bishop to have set foot in Ireland. Prosper of Aquitaine, an advisor to Pope Leo (who long after Patrick's day would send Augustine to Canterbury), noted that a bishop named Palladius had been sent to minister to 'the Irish who believe in Christ'.[56] This phrase suggests that he was serving small but established Christian communities consisting of Romano-British slaves and expatriate merchants who were now living in Ireland. It is thought that Palladius ministered mainly in the South of the island, whereas Patrick's mission was based in the Northwest. Muirchu suggests that Palladius had only a very brief stay in Ireland and states that Patrick's mission began when he received news of Palladius's death. Although the facts are shrouded in mystery, it is clear that Patrick was not the first cleric to minister to the Irish, and

---

[54] *Letter* 26

[55] *Confessio* 50

[56] See Peter Brown, *The Rise of Western Christendom*. Oxford, Blackwell, 2003 p.130.

there may have been a good number who had arrived in Ireland before him, but he was certainly among the most effective.

Patrick's mission had great success against overwhelming odds. He saw thousands come to faith and be baptised. Remarkably, Christianity was tolerated by many in Ireland and, although he faced opposition, there was no sustained persecution of the Church as had taken place elsewhere. Patrick trained and ordained priests to look after his new converts and this enabled him to move on to other areas whilst leaving in capable hands the communities which he had established. In today's parlance, we would describe him as a church planter whose method was to appoint and empower indigenous leaders.[57] Patrick seemed particularly pleased with the fact that he had raised up monks and nuns, writing:

> How has this happened in Ireland? ...the sons and daughters of the leaders of the Irish are seen to be monks and virgins of Christ! [58]

This was a remarkable achievement, since the Irish ruling classes relied on their offspring to provide continuity of rule for their families. Peter Brown expresses the miracle of Patrick's success:

> How had Patricius, a non-Irishman and a Christian, been received into a pagan land... in which social relations were established through the exchange of gifts[?] The Irish insisted on a correct balance of gift and counter-gift. In that case, Christian writers asked, how is it possible that in exchange for no more than a

---

[57] His methods resembled those proposed by Roland Allen in his book *The Spontaneous Expansion of the Church.* Cambridge Lutterworth, 2006; and in *Missionary Methods: St Paul's and Ours.* London, Robert Scott, 2011.

[58] *Confessio* 41

few Latin words of blessing written on pages of white parchment, this Christian stranger could have charmed from so many hard-fisted chieftains so much solid wealth? For Patricius and his successors had been able to receive from the laity of Ireland land, gold, cattle, even their own daughters, as nuns given to Christ? [59]

Alongside this 'spiritual role' we see another strand to Patrick's ministry which was the freeing of slaves, often achieved by paying a ransom to their owners. It is unlikely that a 5th century Christian would have differentiated between a spiritual role and any other endeavour that ensured human flourishing. It was, for Patrick, all part of the package of his ministry as a bishop. His *Letter to the Soldiers of Coroticus* demonstrates how much he abhorred the enslavement of people, and he was especially outraged that raiders who were nominally Christian could enslave or kill fellow Christians.

Patrick's Ecclesial Context

As mentioned above, Christians are divided on the question of the legitimacy of the episcopal system, that is, a hierarchy consisting of archbishops, bishops, priests, and deacons. Catholic, Eastern Orthodox and Episcopalian Churches believe in the validity of this arrangement which became dominant in the 2nd century. At this time, the role of the bishop came to the fore in defending the Church against burgeoning heresies and bishops also provided a rallying point for the faithful in times of persecution. The defenders of an episcopal form of church governance argue that the emergence of this system early in the life of the Church indicates that its historical

---

[59] Brown (2003), p.132-3.

development was intended by God from the outset.

Its detractors tend to see it as developing after the apostolic period in response to particular historical circumstances, regarding it as downplaying the priesthood of all believers and leaving what to them is a lamentable legacy of clergy/laity divide. They argue that Acts portrays a less formally structured set-up consisting of several networks of small home-based churches, each of which related to similar local groups under the care of specific apostolic founding figures; that leading figures came together to discuss the pressing issues of the day, as described in Acts 15, but, this apart, there is little evidence of a more overarching structure. They point out that there is certainly no sense in Paul's writings, for example, that he saw a need to defer to Peter, albeit that he consulted Peter and other prominent leaders.

However we regard the system of bishops – help or hindrance - very few in the Church would deny the need for some sort of recognised leadership and some degree of hierarchy (and we should note that 'hierarchy' literally refers to the leadership in a temple, so has religious connotations). Virtually every Christian denomination or stream has a way of appointing or confirming leaders. In my own Charismatic Church circles, this is very much a process of publicly recognising that God has called someone to leadership, as evidenced by what they are already doing in the Church or some other ministry context. In other perhaps more formal circles, the process often involves the individual him or herself discerning a call and then undergoing a long training process of ministerial formation which includes both academic and practical components.

As far as Patrick was concerned, his confidence was based on the belief that the Lord was the primary mover in the process of conferring on him the role of bishop, and it was certainly not a mere human appointment. This office was perhaps necessary in his ecclesial context as it allowed Patrick himself to ordain Irish priests. The appointment of these leaders and their acceptance by the Church at large was essential for the long-term survival of his mission. They would have been recognised as being legitimate by the wider Church on the basis that they had been appointed by a bishop.

For us, this raises issues as to how much we are helped or hindered by working either within or outside of strongly denominational systems. Although our context is very different from that of Patrick, the same issue of what is best for the success of our mission is what will determine our response to this question. Another factor for us to bear in mind is that of our actual cultural, historical and geographical context. Where society is organised according to strongly hierarchical structures then the exercise of more pronounced and developed power in church leadership is likely not only to be expected but also to be more effective - and the converse is also true. In other words, different contexts require different styles of leadership.

The important point is not whether Patrick was operating within the 'right' ecclesial system but that he regarded his commission as a bishop in the same way that Paul and Peter regarded their apostleship. It was not that they were self-appointed or that an ecclesial committee had chosen them; they were convinced that God himself had appointed them to this office. The Church's role was to *recognise and confirm* what was in essence a call of God.

Authority as a Captive of Christ

Despite his evident sense of loneliness and the opposition he faced, Patrick had huge pride in the fact that God had called him to return to Ireland and that, as stated, he had been appointed a bishop, which itself was confirmation of his call. It is evident that many years had elapsed between Patrick receiving a call and obeying that call and it could be that Muirchu was correct in portraying him as needing to acquire 'divine wisdom'. Patrick must have felt the need to become a bishop before he could fulfil his mission to the Irish, something which would have required a long training, initially as a priest. It is possible that Patrick viewed the completion of his training as a bishop as the sign that he had at last been prepared to undertake his mission.

The practicalities were that in those regions overseen more directly by Rome, a new bishop was conferred in his role by three other bishops. By contrast, the Celtic regions required only one other bishop to appoint someone to this office. This practice, which came to be known as apostolic succession, recognised that ministry is not an individualistic undertaking but that it exists within, and is recognised by, a community of faith. This is similar to the situation described in Paul's letters to Timothy, where leadership was conferred by Paul himself as well as by other leaders (2 Timothy 1:6-7; 1 Timothy 4:4).

Patrick's story illustrates the fact that Christ commissions people and then gives them to his Church, as a gift, to lead and shape it. This is emphasised in Ephesians chapter 4, where the imagery employed partly draws on the familiar scene whereby a returning conquering Roman general is awarded a triumphal entry into the city of Rome, during which ceremony he distributes largesse, including that of captive slaves, to the population. Patrick was one such slave of Christ, given to the (future) Irish Church.

Patrick had returned to Ireland as a captive, not a slave to the Irish but as a willing servant of Christ. He also returned as a bishop with a new sense of authority. This combination of servanthood and authority provided the essentials for a ministry that would survive in the long term. Both elements are crucial now as then and the sense that we are servants of the

Church has to be held alongside those waymarks which indicate that God has called, authorised and equipped us.[60] We are not simply operating out of compassion, our natural concern, seeing a need or a desire to help others. While these are all great motivations for service, on their own they are unlikely to provide us with the confidence needed to survive those times of chaos, upheaval, opposition, anxiety or self-doubt that are inevitably encountered in any form of leadership role. In order to lead both effectively and consistently, we need the conviction not only that we are called and commissioned by God but also that this has been recognised and confirmed in some way by the wider Church.

---

[60] Such as passages of Scripture that have been highlighted to us, words of prophecy or the confirmation of others.

PART 4

CONTEMPORARY LEADERSHIP & SAINT PATRICK

7

Culture

We began our exploration of Patrick's life by considering the bewildering circumstances in which Patrick found himself in both 5th century Britain and Ireland. This chapter sets the scene for the final two sections of the book by exploring the cultural setting which forms the background for contemporary church leadership in the West.

There are inevitably huge differences between our context and that of Patrick, but there is some resonance. The concepts of 'liminality' and 'massive discontinuous change' were used to denote the nature of the challenges which Patrick faced. These terms also aptly describe the shifting sands of Western culture which confront us at the beginning of the 21st century and which form the context for ministry today.

An awareness of our cultural landscape and the effect it has on the Church is vital for effective church leadership. We live in a society where beliefs, mores and values are changing at an increasingly alarming pace and there is frequently the need to rethink how we might best respond to this shift. The phrase 'future shock' was coined in the 1970s to describe the disorientation that such profound cultural change creates, but arguably, in recent years, the rate of change has accelerated considerably and we now face an ever more far-reaching transformation of the nature of society.

Our Cultural Landscape

The role of the Church in today's society is largely appreciated especially with regard to social issues. Many town and city councils in the UK turn to local church 'Street Pastors' to make their streets safe at night and to provide support for young people who might otherwise be more vulnerable. In addition, many people draw on church-run foodbanks and receive debt counselling, but in terms of ideology the Christian faith is, in fact, no longer a dominant force to be reckoned with in Western society. Its power is waning, and its voice is less heeded. In many countries we find ourselves to be in a distinct minority. We face new challenges as Christian orthodoxy is less welcome in the public arena and is frequently regarded as being outmoded and irrelevant to the issues of the day.

The reasons behind this shift are complex. For many, scientific explanations have replaced religious theology and understanding, and this fact, together with incredulous dismay and even horror at the words and actions of religious fundamentalists, has contributed to the increasing abandonment of religious faith. Historically, the challenge to faith brought about by two world wars is thought to have been particularly significant in Church decline in the UK. Anecdotally, the current ongoing news of deeply disturbing and unending conflict in war-torn regions around the world is currently raising similar challenges to belief in a loving God.

Added to this, it is certainly true that a number of recent high-profile scandals have contributed to a tarnishing of the Church's reputation and the politicization of some sections of the Church has not helped either. However, the major roots of the current crisis for the Church are largely external and relate more to wider societal forces which stretch back over many decades, rather than to anything we as Christians may have done. Some in the West, such as the New Atheists, promote a radically anti-religious agenda but, paradoxically, others have embraced a mixture of vague 'spirituality' often combined with self-help psychology, which focuses on the individual and his or her own experience.

For those who identify as 'spiritual but not religious', truth is often viewed as being subjective, more in terms of a personal possession, 'my truth', rather than being external and objective, such as is found in the historic Christian creeds. Increasingly, Christian leaders vie with a thousand other voices that clamour for attention. We are no longer automatically accorded a hearing and our authority – both personal and corporate – has been weakened. These and many other such factors (such as the current debate around gender fluidity for example) present a real challenge to those in leadership.

The fact that Church decline, as in the 5th century, is largely the result of factors outside our control means that church leaders now find themselves in a seemingly relatively powerless position. There is no obvious strategy presenting itself to reverse the wider societal trends which continue to have such an impact on the Church. Even though we may be able to influence them to a limited extent in particular places, many of these changes represent global shifts way beyond our ability to affect. This situation can only be faced if we are willing to re-examine the assumptions, as well as the imagination, that underlie how we perceive our role. Our new cultural landscape can be difficult to come to terms with and many leaders act as if continuing as before with redoubled effort will rectify the situation, whereas, in fact, a different approach altogether is almost certainly needed.

Church Culture

> As Christians, we are often unaware that our beliefs are shaped more by our culture than by the gospel.
> PAUL HIEBERT [61]

These cultural shifts also raise the question of how the Church should relate to the surrounding culture. This was the question addressed by H. Richard Niebuhr in his classic book *Christ and Culture*, first published in 1951.[62] Niebuhr outlines six possible ways in which we can position ourselves with regards to the surrounding culture. More recently Hiebert has also addressed this topic and his astute observation, quoted above, highlights a crucial issue for us to consider as church leaders: what does it require for our churches to become genuine Christian communities which are distinctive, yet which prepare people to be both 'in' but at the same time 'not of' the world? This is not always easy to achieve and Paul Hiebert flagged up our current tendency towards the 'of the world' option.

On the other hand, it is important not to create insular Christian subcultures which might mean that while we avoid worldliness we are scarcely actually 'in the world'. Such subcultures can be very engrossing and being involved in them can be viewed as a sign of radical commitment. Yet they rarely equip individuals to develop friendships with unchurched neighbours or colleagues, which as genuine relationships form the context in which acts of mercy or opportunities for sharing faith might occur naturally.

The process of reimagining leadership is helped if we can take a long in-depth look at the culture of our churches and

---

[61] Paul Hiebert, *The Gospel in Human Contexts: Anthropological Explorations for Contemporary Missions.* Grand Rapids, Baker, 2009, p.18.

[62] H. Richard Niebuhr, *Christ and Culture.* San Francisco, Harper Collins, 2001.

consider what might need to change. It is not always easy to be clear about the sort of church cultures that are conducive to making effective disciples and those which might hamper this task, but creating a healthy church culture starts with fostering within our congregations or organisation an imagination of what this might entail in our particular contexts.

Social scientists describe culture as encompassing the beliefs, worldview, behavioural patterns and practices of a civilisation – more colloquially, we can say that culture is 'just the way things are done around here'.[63] This social scientific concept of culture can be applied to society as a whole, but it can also be used to describe the beliefs and practices of subgroups within society. Similarly, families also have their own unique cultures: for example, in one family work is regarded as the means to provide finance for the necessities of life and to be able to afford enjoyable experiences, whereas in another family work is primarily a signifier of status and offspring are pushed towards high prestige professions such as law or medicine. Some families have a very ordered, more formal, culture while others might foster spontaneity and enjoy a slightly chaotic atmosphere.

Certain aspects of Western culture, such as expectations with respect to sexual behaviour, are at odds with what is generally expected in the Church but, in addition, denominations and local churches establish their own cultural norms to which members are expected, albeit in unspoken ways, to conform. These expectations may be stated but many are unwritten and new members simply imbibe the way things are done. Individual churches establish their distinctive cultural norms, such as how to dress for Sunday worship, whether people should tithe a certain proportion of their income, or whether silence or being more expressive in worship signals

---

[63] Explored further in Hiebert (2009) p.150-9.

devotion to God. It is easy to spot the culture of very distinctive religious groups, such as the Amish, but it is less easy to be aware of the nature of our own church culture simply because it is more familiar to us and we generally accept it as being normal. As an insider in a particular society or group, the accepted cultural mores seem both natural and self-evident, and we are often unaware that we even have these unwritten rules as to what is good, bad, or even taboo.

If we have been a member of a church for many years, we are likely to be unaware of many aspects of our church's culture, reminiscent of the joke where one goldfish asks another, 'How's the water?' The other fish replies, 'What's water?' Because our environment, our 'water', is taken for granted it can be difficult to describe it to others, and it can be particularly difficult to critique our church culture if we are surrounded by like-minded people. This is, of course, one of the dangers of social media as algorithms direct us towards others with similar views to our own and these echo chambers only reinforce our views.

It is important to have contact with people from other (to us more alien) cultures as this makes us aware that not everyone sees our culture as being the best on offer. An example of this is a friend's story of how an African pastor staying with him had eventually taken him aside to express his shock that Christians in the West allow elderly relatives to go into residential homes, rather than being looked after by their own families, as was the custom in his own society. The point is not that one approach is right and the other wrong, but that only by stepping outside our cultural framework can we hope to gain a clearer view.

Insular Christian Subcultures

If we are to be faithful to Scripture, the Church must be counter-cultural in certain respects, such as resisting materialism and promiscuity, countering the exploitation of the vulnerable and so on. It takes a strong counter-cultural Christian community to form disciples in the way of Jesus and the formation of such communities is a principal task of leadership. Yet the role of a community, like that of a home (physical or spiritual), is to prepare offspring for the big wide world and to cultivate those qualities that will ensure a productive engagement with those outside of our home environment.

The goal of creating communities of faith which enable people to engage in mission (in the broadest sense of the term) is subverted if we simply create self-contained worlds that allow Christians to exist in a bubble with little contact with those in the dominant culture around us. In reaction to the confusion created by the many unwelcome changes in wider society, some in our churches have done just this and 'pulled up the drawbridge' to retreat into Christian subcultures, which, in effect, are ghettos. It is, for example, possible to listen to Christian music, socialise only with friends from our church and for life to revolve entirely around Church activities to the extent that we forget how to have anything more than a superficial conversation with unchurched friends or neighbours, as we have very little in common. In short, in some cases, we are in danger of losing our natural connections with people around us. As Os Guinness lamented, we can unwittingly create a 'privately engaging, publicly irrelevant' faith.

In this regard, we noted Patrick's engagement with the surrounding society as he worked to free slaves. This was an example of missional engagement with the practical needs of those in need within the communities he was seeking to reach. Also, it may have been significant that his mission was in the context of small communities and that those in the churches he founded would for economic, security and social reasons necessarily have continued to be involved in their tribe or village. In Patrick's setting there were simply insufficient numbers of believers to create self-contained units; structures which would effectively have abstracted out those who had come to faith in separate spiritual silos with little contact with those around them. Encouragingly, we can draw inspiration from the rootedness of Patrick's new converts and churches within their localities, as it allowed those involved to maintain and form natural, normal connections and associations with family, friends, neighbours and fellow workers. Even when we consider the later creation of widespread monastic structures, their rootedness in their locality, as centres of art, hospitality and spiritual direction, was also a fundamental element in their success.

Rootedness

Missiologists Hirsch and Frost stress the importance of this 'real and abiding presence among a group of people'.[64] In a similar vein, Van Gelder and Zscheile highlight the need for us to engage with and participate in society rather than forming a counter society which, even if it seeks to create structures that serve the needs of society, is liable to become paternalistic in its approach and attitude to those being served:

> Missional church cannot participate in God's passion for the world without drawing close to its neighbours... surrendering a posture of control, distance and mere benevolence in order to enter closely into relational community.[65]

---

[64] See: Michael Frost and Alan Hirsch, *The Shaping of Things to Come: Innovation and Mission for the 21st Century.* Peabody, Hendrickson, 2003, p.39.

[65] Craig Van Gelder and Dwight Zscheile, *The Missional Church in Perspective.* Grand Rapids, Baker Academic, 2011, p.115.

My own experience of church leadership has mainly been in the context of two rural churches which I helped plant. The first was in a village which met on a Sunday in a rented school hall and gymnasium. Despite being a small church, we were very active in our community, at one time running two separate youth clubs, church groups for both young people and adults, a parent and toddler group and, occasionally, an Alpha Course. Every summer we would also run an activities week for school children. While there was much good that came out of these activities and some lasting fruit, we were, however, very busy!

Once we had moved to another small town, we also found ourselves moving away from this more 'attractional' approach to be less activist in terms of developing church-run projects. Instead, we simply became involved as individuals, or groups of individuals, with already existing activities in the local community, which we ourselves, in the main, were not actually running or managing. For some this involved helping with the local food bank or teaching refugees or providing accommodation for them – while for others this mainly meant joining clubs and societies or getting involved in the local music scene. What has been of special note is that this was not, at any point, promoted as a strategy. It simply evolved as people in the church pursued either what they felt drawn to by God or what they enjoyed doing in terms of leisure pursuits, hobbies and interests.

What we have noticed is that whereas conversations about faith were quite rare in our previous setting, they are now much more common and arise quite spontaneously. In fact, many of these conversations are initiated by others who, because they have got to know us and know of our Christian faith, may simply wish to talk about their own approach to spirituality or to explore Christianity a little further through conversation.

In our first situation, clearly we were serving our local

community, but with little time available to join local clubs or to interact with neighbours in other ways (an exception being that I would often chat with my next-door neighbour as we hung out together in our garages pretending to look busy!) Yet the key to effective missional church involves being 'incarnational', living in the neighbourhood and engaging with it. This undoubtedly includes the development of genuine relationships and friendships with those outside our circle, friendships in which we both give *and receive* support.

Having already noted that many people with whom we have contact are actively exploring or are immersed in New Age beliefs or neopaganism, anecdotally we have found that paradoxically this is not altogether negative as many are very open to talking about Christianity. The challenge is then to create both the time and the mental space to engage meaningfully with those who want to explore further. Involvement in fewer specifically Christian settings and projects not only releases more time and energy, but also creates more space for prayer.

I am not suggesting that Christian projects are in any way wrong; just the reverse, in fact, as they provide forums for us, both to work with individuals from other churches as well as with those outside the Church, to serve our communities. But what I am seeking to highlight is the need to consider the observations of Frost, Hirsch, etc concerning the dangers of 'abstracting out' those in our churches from 'normal' society by promoting an overly activist and attractional, as opposed to an incarnational, approach.

Developing a Real-World Faith

Consideration of the dangers inherent in creating a Christian subculture or abstracting church members from their communities in other ways may help us address the vexed question as to why so many of our young people drift away from faith when they go to college or start work. One proposed way ahead has been to ensure that there are enough small groups in local churches, colleges, workplaces and other spaces to support Christians from the cradle to the grave. That is one possible solution, although it fails to address the issue of why so many young people, who have been exposed to hundreds of hours of sermons and numerous church groups, wither in the wider world.

It may be that we are good at equipping young people to survive in church culture, but less so with respect to the dominant secular culture. We need to ask some tough questions, such as why our processes of inculturation as good church members may not necessarily produce the sort of real-world resilience we witnessed in Patrick's life. There are no easy answers to this question.

We have seen that Patrick himself was raised in a Christian environment and that, initially, this actually had little apparent impact on his life. Interestingly, it was only in the experience of adversity that he developed a faith robust enough to survive in the world outside his early more sheltered setting. This dynamic resonates with the work of Victor Turner who studied particular African tribes which initiated young men into manhood through circumcision followed by being abandoned as a group in the desert or jungle. Up to that point their experience had been one of being nurtured and cared for, but now they had to learn how to survive against the odds. It was, in fact, Turner who coined the term *liminality*, as considered earlier, to describe this process of being pushed to the extreme limits of endurance and tolerance.

There may be lessons here for us today and perhaps we should consider the value of creating intentional liminal experiences for teens and young adults, as well as for older Christians who might benefit from the experience of being placed in faith-stretching contexts. This might, for example, involve a *Youth With A Mission* gap year or taking people on short-term mission trips to the developing world. Being out of our comfort zone can develop resilience and, as with Patrick, being cut off from our usual mechanisms for support can increase our capacity to trust God.

Churches often (rightly) provide nurture but can overlook the formative potential of exposure to challenge and a certain amount of risk. Alan Hirsch points out that when people experience liminal situations together, this creates *communitas*, a term that signifies that those involved have become participants in koinonia, a shared life, a band of brothers.[66] The concept of communitas takes that of community one significant step further since the creation of communitas involves people actually being forged together through the challenges faced and undertaken together. In this way, and through such formative experiences, those involved come to strongly identify with their (Christian) tribe and culture and, no doubt, are even more likely to do so with the realisation of its resilience in the face of real-life and real-world challenges.

In fact, whether we have young or more mature Christians in view, rather than somewhat artificially seeking to create experiences for ourselves to enhance and promote 'communitas', it may be that as we increasingly face being side-lined or are even subjected to open hostility and discrimination, 'communitas' naturally develops as a direct consequence. Indeed, this has been the case throughout the ages whenever the Church is subject to persecution.

---

[66] Alan Hirsch, *The Forgotten Ways: Reactivating the Missional Church*. Grand Rapids, Brazos Press, 2006, chapter 8.

8

Cul-de-sacs

> CUL-DE-SAC: a dead-end street; any situation in which further progress is impossible.[67]

As Paul Hiebert alluded to, Western culture inevitably affects the values of those in and of those who lead the Church, as well as offering models of leadership that reflect those values. Some of these models are based upon realistic expectations of leaders and allow for our human frailty. Others are far less realistic, particularly those which promote the sort of leadership that is primarily based on creating a positive public image dependent mainly on personal charisma. This style of leadership is increasingly common in the internet age and although seemingly holding much promise, it inevitably turns out to be a cul-de-sac. For those in the Church who might be influenced by this model of leadership, there is engagement, albeit unwittingly, with the celebrity culture we see so often portrayed in the media and constantly reinforced on social media platforms. The result is a Christianised version of this all-too-familiar milieu.

The rise of this kind of personality-based leadership is evidenced not just on social media, but also on podcasts, the

---

[67] https://www.dictionary.com/browse/cul-de-sac

Christian music scene and in the existence of what are in effect celebrity pastors. The quest to find an idealised heroic leader is one understandable response to the rising tide of atheism, agnosticism, and New Age beliefs. We may believe that the solution to the bewildering state of affairs we see around us is to find a charismatic leader who can act on our behalf. It can be the case that God Himself raises up leaders, often reluctant figures like many we read of in Scripture, such as Jonah, Gideon, even Moses.

But sometimes church leaders themselves aspire to heroic leadership because they are driven by a high need for recognition, some with deep character flaws which subsequently come to light. By way of contrast, we have seen that Patrick was clear that he was the least of Christians and that he certainly did not show evidence of a saviour complex. Such humility and realism concerning our own personal weakness is the main way in which we can resist the seductive forces of the need for recognition and significance. Yet adulation is powerful and incredibly difficult to ignore. Even Jesus experienced a major challenge to overcome this particular temptation in the wilderness. The Jesus Prayer from Eastern Orthodoxy ('Lord Jesus Christ, Son of God, have mercy on me, a sinner') is particularly helpful in this respect and can ground us in reality, limiting the scope for entertaining an unreal, distorted view of ourselves.

Grandiose notions of ourselves can also easily flourish in grandiose settings, like huge stadiums and concert halls used for Christian gatherings of various kinds. In the first Christian centuries, churches were predominantly home-based and even with the emergence of specialised church buildings, congregations would still have been small enough to maintain a family feel. In most cases, Christian leaders would have been personally known by those they led and were experienced in the warp and woof of everyday ordinary life. The setting, as well as the size, of congregations today can easily distance leaders from people in their churches and circles. When this occurs, being somewhat removed is conducive for idealisation by others to occur.

Yet even in the context of the home churches he founded, Paul had to warn against the emergence of outwardly impressive 'super-apostles' who were focused on gaining financial support and wanted to have a personal following. The style of leadership they offered contrasted with that of Paul whose humble demeanour and evident lack of charisma or physical presence were regarded by some as evidence of ineffectiveness. It appeared that he had poor 'stage presence' and lacked the highly polished rhetorical skills that were expected of public figures, philosophers and religious teachers (2 Corinthians 10:10 & 11:5-9). Later Christian writings warn against the possibility of *unknown* itinerant apostles and prophets exploiting local congregations.[68] If idealisation and/or exploitation was such a danger in Paul's day, how much more, in an age of social media, where image is so often valued over substance, should we be on our guard?

Personality-Centred Leadership

> The wicked leader is despised by the people, the good leader is revered, but when a great leader leads, the people say 'we did it ourselves'.

These words of Lao Tzu (450 BC) suggest that over the longer term, leaders who remain in the background are likely to be more effective than those who aspire to be in the foreground. If Lao Tzu is correct, the most successful leaders are those who empower others to such an extent that the leader's own

---

[68] See *The Didache*, written sometime between 80 and 120 AD.

contribution to the success of the group or its task will most likely be overlooked or forgotten. This is in keeping with several passages in the New Testament where the emphasis is on the sort of leadership that enables others to discover and operate in their gifts and calling (Ephesians 4:7-16) and where serving others is valued over prominence (Matthew 20:26).

Despite the clear biblical injunctions and exhortations, the idealisation of prominent Christian leaders is common today. Yet this is not altogether new, and the Charismatic wing of the Church (with which I am associated) has always, albeit unconsciously, tended to look to leaders who have an impressive stage presence with the necessary rhetorical skills to challenge, motivate, inspire, and mobilise the Church. Such people were once referred to as 'God's Man of Power for the Hour' - and it was usually a *man* who was considered to be worthy of being placed on a pedestal!

There are, of course, times when more prominent - 'heroic' – leaders are essential, such as in times of war or crisis. The concept of heroic leadership has a long history, and we think particularly of great men and women such as Moses, who led Israel at a time of crisis, as well as of Boudicca, the mythical King Arthur, and more recently, despite their well-documented flaws, Winston Churchill and Martin Luther King Jr.[69] However, some suggest that our current cultural moment requires those who can mobilise and empower others by facilitating the development of their gifts and encouraging what has been termed their 'missional imagination' rather than looking to heroic leaders.[70] Effective leaders are usually the ground crew

---

[69] We should also note that Adolf Hitler came to power in the guise of a heroic leader, so in and of itself heroic leadership is not always good news.

[70] See Alan Roxburgh, *The Sky is Falling: Leaders Lost in Transition*. Eagle, ID, ACI Publishing, 2005, p.145-7. Michael Frost and Alan Hirsch, *The Shaping of Things to Come: Innovation and Mission for the 21st Century*. Peabody, Hendrickson, 2003, chapter 11.

often found working behind the scenes, rather than those flying the fighter planes.

That said, liminal situations do create the pressure for leaders to be exceptional or heroic, and it is understandable that once a measure of success is achieved, leaders may be regarded as such by others. There are a number of compelling reasons to gently disavow any such accolades as the negative consequences of personality-centred leadership highlight only too well; these reasons include the following:

1. PERSONALITY-BASED LEADERSHIP ENCOURAGES NARCISSISM

Full-blown narcissistic personality disorder (NPD) is not common in Christian leaders, although many of us do exhibit some more minor NPD traits, as would be expected in any sample of the general population.

Some years ago, to heighten self-awareness for church leaders, I used a self-analysis questionnaire based on personality disorders. We all have some degree of dysfunction, and although this was of necessity a naming exercise, it was not a blaming exercise.

The three most common dysfunctional personality clusters reported were:

- Traits indicating a degree of *co-dependent personality disorder*. This is where we actively need others to be needy so that we can care for them in order to feel good about ourselves. In this case, we tend to keep others dependent on our help rather than empowering them to help themselves – hence, the term 'co-dependency' – the helped person needs us and we, in turn, need them.

- *Paranoid traits* whereby we find it difficult to believe that others have our best interests at heart but think rather that they represent a threat or competition. This sometimes is evidenced when there is suspicion present in leaders' attitudes towards others, with the result that it drives those leaders affected towards isolation and a critical attitude develops to those 'not of us'.

- *Narcissistic traits* with a high need to be admired and recognised as being special. If we score above average for NPD traits, we tend to actively seek such recognition, we desire prominence and want to make a name for ourselves.

I possess some traits of all three of these most common dysfunctionalities, and it is useful to be aware of our own profile so that we can moderate the expression of these negative motivators in our lives.

Narcissism is a popular topic on YouTube and is certainly over diagnosed by amateur psychologists, to the extent that anyone whose behaviour is not liked can be labelled as being narcissistic. Those with narcissistic traits, when genuinely present, often feel that they are being overlooked. When accolades are received, however, they never quite heal the inner wound which underlies narcissism and, despite any achievements, more acknowledgement is still needed from others to authenticate the person's sense of worth.[71] In fact, all three of these dysfunctional personality clusters are related to issues of insecurity.

Several prominent church leaders have recently been shown to have serious shadow sides to their characters and it is worth considering whether the very experience of being repeatedly applauded and acclaimed is more than many can handle (there are, fortunately, notable exceptions, such as Billy Graham). My own experience of a number of gifted leaders suggests that there may be an unhelpful dynamic at play here

---

[71] Of course, there is a healthier form of narcissism, whereby we regard ourselves as being the recipient of other's love and care, but without seeing ourselves as being a special case.

whereby already existing, though minor, narcissistic traits become magnified once prominence is achieved and recognition leads to adulation, so feeding the narcissism.

It also seems to be the case that being regarded as special in some way tends to make some people feel that the normal rules of behaviour, including the need to respect others' autonomy, no longer apply to them. The followers of such leaders often overlook character flaws or actual wrongdoing 'for the sake of the ministry' or because the leader in question is notably gifted. Gifted leaders are then regarded as being exempt from what is expected of every church member in terms of transparency, openness, accountability and the need sometimes to apologise and admit wrongdoing.

There can be a degree almost of worship that occurs when it is believed that certain individuals possess innate gifts of such value that they are regarded as being somehow indispensable to God's work. This is reminiscent of the way in which Paul and Barnabas, having performed a miracle in Lystra, were regarded by people as being gods (Acts 18:8-18). The person him or herself may then also fall prey to such erroneous thinking and so the myth is perpetuated. Patrick, by contrast, attributed any success he had to God's grace alone, rather than to any personal qualities he possessed:

> I didn't deserve at all that the Lord would grant such great grace, after hardships and troubles, after captivity, and after so many years among that people.[72]

He clearly felt unworthy, and his example suggests that the best course of action is to regard ourselves and, therefore, to present ourselves to others as the fallible and flawed beings we are in reality. The Jungian concept of the wounded healer, though regarded as unhelpful by some, has, I believe, much

---

[72] *Confessio* 15

merit in reigning in any tendency we might have towards narcissism and in acknowledging that we too are flawed and wounded.

2. PERSONALITY-BASED LEADERSHIP IGNORES THE IMPORTANCE OF PROXIMITY

Personality-based leaders are usually distant figures with whom people in their churches or their followers have little personal connection or contact. In addition, such leaders often do not allow themselves to be known well even by those deemed as friends or by those who are walking alongside them. An image of competence is projected often using well-crafted publicity, and giving an altogether wholesome profile, yet maintaining a measured distance from those they lead. While it can be tempting to project an image of strength and competence, there is the ever-present danger of believing your own publicity! But, as we have seen, this directly contrasts with Patrick's emphasis on his sinfulness, his perceived lack of innate suitability for ministry and his utter reliance on the fact that God had called and credentialled him for service in Ireland.

Paul's apostolic ministry was, in fact, characterised by proximity rather than distance, evidenced by the familial terms he used to describe the intimate nature of his relationship with those in the churches he founded - even on one occasion describing himself as having been a nursing mother to them (1 Thessalonians 2:7). Patrick was similarly sacrificial, willing to put himself at great risk for the sake of those to whom he ministered: 'I spend myself for you that you may have me for yours'.[73]

Despite his wide influence, his writing emphasises the importance of being embedded in community and of being known personally: 'You all know, and God knows, how I have

---

[73] *Confessio* 51

lived among you from my youth...'[74] Clearly, for those who lead large churches or organisations this presents some challenges as we can only meaningfully relate to a relatively small number of people. Hence, there is the need to actively foster relationships with particular individuals or groups of friends where we are regarded in a realistic manner - neither held in awe, nor seen as needing to meet some unrealistic standard.

3. PERSONALITY-BASED LEADERSHIP OFTEN SIDESTEPS THE NEED FOR ACCOUNTABILITY

In order to maintain an attitude of humility, it is helpful if we invite specific people to offer constructive criticism, and this is perhaps best done by having a group of peers who not only care for us but who are also able to be honest with us. Most dysfunctional behaviour develops gradually, by degrees, rather than suddenly. Knowing that we are committed to being open and honest with a few selected people is a great spur to keep 'short accounts' with God and to correct any unhelpful traits early on in our development.

A group to whom we are accountable can also help us to evaluate any harsher critical voices. We are aware that people can, usually unconsciously, attempt to work through their childhood issues possibly involving, for example, failure of care or abusive authority figures, in their current relationship with a leader. Stories abound of Christian leaders who have been subjected to unfair criticism, and I know some who have had serious breakdowns as a result. Since at times a particular criticism may be justified, a more objective view can be gained if we have others with whom we can talk about such things, people who know us well enough to be aware of our feet of clay but who also are conversant with the dynamic described above.

---

[74] *Confessio* 48

A teaching promulgated in some Charismatic circles goes under the title of 'creating a culture of honour'. This phrase, used outside the Church, has several meanings. In the Southern USA it refers to the kindness involved in avoiding causing distress to others through our words and actions. In the Middle East, it is associated with responding to offence, particularly against the family, with violence. It has also recently been used by churches and although this term rightly emphasises the fact that we need to avoid a critical attitude towards leaders, the 'culture of honour' teaching is being widely promoted to avoid any legitimate critique or indeed criticism of high-profile leaders. There have been examples where this teaching has been used to avoid leaders being held accountable by actually silencing dissenting voices in the congregation.

The Reality of Leadership

Patrick's *Confession* illustrates the fact that leadership is often very much harder than it looks from the outside. Being candid about our fallibility, our anxiety and the reality of leadership is important for many reasons. One is that such honesty can help those who follow us in leadership to avoid disillusionment when the reality of church life doesn't match up to the imagined ideal.

In contrast to Patrick's own account of his life, Muirchu's biography begins by expanding on Patrick's own account, filling in plausible details, but then, somewhat disappointingly and decidedly unrealistically, goes on to paint a picture of Patrick as a superhero.[75] This image portrays Patrick as powerfully cursing his enemies and causing darkness to fall so that his opponents end up mistakenly killing one another. He

---

[75] Muirchu's *Life* 17, 18, 20, 24.

is pictured as calling down snow and causes the pirate Coroticus to turn into a fox. This account, of course, sharply contrasts with the reality of what we actually know of Patrick's lived experience. Muirchu's Patrick exhibited boundless confidence but the real Patrick admitted to anxiety for his safety and needed to draw on the resilience he had developed in facing past challenges.

For a realistic account of church leadership, I would recommend David Hansen's book *The Art of Pastoring*. [76] It is a beautiful account of ministry which celebrates the quiet victories achieved through faithful pastoral practice in rural Montana, including his ministry to people he met through his hobby of fly fishing (a very different setting, of course, from Patrick's context).

The quest for leaders who have life and ministry all sorted inevitably leads to disillusionment. If proximity to such people is achieved, the realisation usually dawns that the wizard at the end of the Yellow Brick Road has no special powers after all. Undoubtedly, Patrick was used by God but the picture he presents is one of having to constantly deal with hardship, trials and challenges, including that of being rejected by his peers. Patrick's own account emphasises the importance of perseverance and endurance in the face of these and other ordeals and sufferings, rather than of any innate or even God-given giftedness he possessed.

---

[76] David Hansen, *The Art of Pastoring: Ministry Without all the Answers*. Downers Grove, IVP, 1994.

PART 5

FINAL THOUGHTS

9

Culmination

In the final sections of his *Confession*, without a hint of grandiosity or self-congratulation, Patrick outlined in a very straightforward manner some of his achievements in Ireland and also described how he had travelled 'even to the furthest parts where nobody lived beyond, and where nobody ever went to baptise and to ordain clerics'.[77] Towards the end of his life, Patrick was able to look back in a realistic way and see that his labour had not been in vain. He recounted his successes in order to defend his ministry against its critics rather than doing so as an exercise in self-glorification.

Patrick's hard work and persistence, often against the backdrop of opposition and insecurity, had a lasting effect and, despite his uncertainty concerning the longevity of his churches, Patrick's legacy is well known. Even today most Irish citizens identify as being Catholic.[78] The extent of Patrick's geographical reach, however, was less than has been claimed by some and it is likely that his influence, though undoubtedly of huge importance, was geographically limited, possibly confined to the northern half of the island.[79]

---

[77] *Confessio* 51

[78] According to the 2022 census, 69% of Irish people are Catholics.

[79] See O'Loughlin (1999), p.31-2 and Haykin (2014), p.77.

The northern city of Armagh is regarded as the ecclesiastical capital of Ireland and legend has it that Patrick established a church there. The Book of Armagh contains Muirchu's account of Patrick's life, and it is likely that emphasising the association of the city with Patrick was a means of increasing its prestige in Ireland at that time. In fact, the establishment of the Church in Ireland was not achieved through Patrick's labours alone, but there is little doubt that he played a highly significant role in establishing a firm foundation for the Irish Church.

Evaluating our Ministry

Using his own account, as well as our awareness of the honour which later churchmen accorded him, we can evaluate several aspects of Patrick's ministry, even if our ability to do so is somewhat limited. Having briefly mentioned some of Patrick's achievements, I aim to explore the topic of how we might actually evaluate the success of our own ministry. This topic is rarely addressed, but is not unimportant since, for many of us, our sense of worth is linked to what we feel God has achieved through us.

Stories of success, like that of Patrick, can be daunting if our own achievements are less spectacular and we, of course, usually compare ourselves with those we deem to be more successful than ourselves. Statistically, it is likely that some of us will compare favourably with our peers and some less favourably! In the context of the marginalisation and overall decline of the Church, we are doing well if we maintain our current numbers. To enable congregations to survive is to swim against the tide of decline, although our hope and intention is to do better than mere maintenance and survival.

Comparison with the ministry of others may inevitably leave us feeling disheartened, but there are some paradoxically comforting facts for those of us who feel we might have less to celebrate. There is, for example, the fact that Jesus' entire church, before Pentecost, was small and could fit into one large room (Acts 1:15 and 2:1). In addition, many of the churches founded and faithfully tended as fledgling communities by Paul were also small home-based churches. Furthermore, the biblical narrative describes how Moses, a leader par excellence, managed to safely deliver only two of those who left Egypt into the Promised Land; statistically a poor outcome for forty years of faithful ministry.

Of course, impact can be difficult to assess unless we rely on metrics such as the size of a church, the number of people baptised or confirmed, books sold, conferences spoken at, etc. It is probably healthy for us to admit that our motives are often mixed, and that according to such criteria we want to do well. Personally, I would like to be a best-selling author as it would boost my morale considerably(!) but, with perhaps a purer motive, I often pray that each book will be helpful to its reader. Of course, our assessment of the fruit of our labours is likely to reflect our tendency towards either optimism or pessimism, and the true and real valuation lies in God's hands.

Outcome

As far as Patrick was concerned, dogged perseverance resulted in fruitfulness, but despite his remarkable success in several areas, Patrick was still anxious about the survival of the Irish churches. He felt that if he had left Ireland to visit friends and family his work would not endure in the longer term, stating: 'I fear the loss of the work I have begun here'.[80] He was also concerned that temptation to sin would get the better of him and wrote that his only hope was the fact that God was

---

[80] *Confessio* 43

Culmination

actively guarding him from evil.[81] Again, this may reflect a tendency towards melancholy but his concern seems genuine. We are aware that many who start well fail to complete the course, so Patrick's sentiment seems to be tinged with healthy realism.

In this regard, it is important to acknowledge that some aspects of Patrick's ministry were actually less successful, such as the introduction of the continental structure of a bishop-led church to Ireland. Although the system of bishops continued, it was the monasteries that proved to be the real powerhouses of Celtic Christianity. This was not, as has been supposed, due to the mythical Irish bias against hierarchy but was related to the absence of large conurbations required to form the seat of a bishop. We should note that, 'Monastic life flourished in Ireland after Patrick's time, but bishops also played a prominent role in the work of the church.'[82] The Irish population, in fact, was distributed mainly among rural settlements, which as local centres were the perfect niches for monasteries to flourish.

Although Patrick had a very high regard for monastic vocation, those who became monks and 'virgins of Christ' under Patrick's leadership probably pursued these callings one by one, mainly as solitary individuals, or in small groups. It fell to his successors to gather these ones and twos into communities and to create the monasteries which we now associate with early Christianity in Ireland. Patrick excelled in his mission, but even so, he was just one link in a chain stretching down the centuries and, in so many ways, his story reminds us of the need for sober evaluation of any influence we may have personally.

---

[81] *Confessio* 43-4

[82] Donald Meek, *The Quest for Celtic Christianity*. Edinburgh, Handsel Press, 2000, p.133.

Many smaller chapels existed alongside the monasteries and in these settings it was priests, rather than monks, who provided pastoral leadership. These figures are less well known than the 'saints' but we should acknowledge the vital role they played. These unknown, often obscure leaders, who achieved less than the more well-known abbots and abbesses, were perhaps the real heroes of 5th century Ireland. They exemplified the words attributed to Count Zinzendorf, 'Preach the gospel, die, and be forgotten'. Many of us will similarly work in obscurity without human recognition or acclaim. Faithfulness and fruit bearing are the issue rather than whether our ministry is recognised.

Bearing Fruit

Too much emphasis on achieving success is unhealthy, particularly if the metrics listed earlier become all-consuming, as we may then be tempted to compromise or even try to modify our calling to ensure better results. I have felt called to rural church ministry and, at times, it has been attractive to relocate to a larger town where a larger church might grow in a more densely populated setting.

If we are overly concerned about our impact, it may be that we are simply unaware of the effect we have had on others. Paul could hardly have realised that his letters, essentially a by-product of his ministry at the time, written to the churches he founded would have such a major impact on the Church down the centuries. If we are faithful and persist, the outcome of our ministry is, in the final analysis, wholly in God's hands (1 Corinthians 3:6). It also appears that the plumbline by which Jesus evaluates impact is not the size of our church but whether there is evidence of care for the poor, the hungry, the sick and those in prison. The story told in Matthew 25:35-40 suggests that this is mainly done unconsciously with the motivation being genuine care for others rather than desire to prove effectiveness.

A useful exercise is to reflect on those who have helped us personally and in so doing myself I realise that some of those who have had the greatest impact on my life would not be deemed 'significant' by many. I can think of Brian and Mary who invited me into their home soon after I came to faith and with whom I learned to pray before we delivered an evangelistic newspaper to their unchurched neighbours. They were probably unaware of the extent to which that experience and their example were formative.

The fruit of our lives has more to do with exhibiting kindness, generosity and gentleness than in assessing the impact we might have in terms of quantifiable success (Galatians 5:22-23). It is the 'good and faithful' servant whom Jesus regarded as successful and he was clearly unimpressed by those, perhaps more outwardly productive people, who performed mighty acts such as healing, but who lacked an active relationship with God (Matthew 25:31). Those whom Jesus 'never knew' were effectively religious technocrats who knew how to do all the right things, pull all the right levers, and to impress the crowd (Matthew 7:22). The fact that they could be productive but not walk with God demonstrates that the work of the Lord can easily come to overshadow the Lord of the work.

Jesus declared that if we abide in him and his word in us, we will bear much fruit and the term 'abide' highlights the centrality of faithfulness. It is also the case that after pruning there is a time-lapse before new growth and fruit appear. We are unlikely to bear much fruit in terms of external impact in a period of intense personal formation when we are being pruned for greater growth. But such times are part of what it means to abide in the Vine, to learn to act in love and to obey his commandments in times of temptation or hardship.

According to Jesus, the practice of abiding in him, even when we experience the stripping away that pruning involves, will certainly lead to fruitfulness in the long term (John 15:1-17). Abiding is another way of telling us to stick with it during those periods of difficulty that under God's hand are essential for our personal formation.

Formation is a Key Issue

> Not only this, but we also rejoice in our sufferings, knowing that suffering produces perseverance; and perseverance, proven character; and proven character, hope; and hope does not disappoint us, because God's love has been poured into our hearts through the Holy Spirit who was given to us.
> ROMANS 5:3-5

We have seen that the circumstances of Patrick's life were not what we might consider to be the ideal context for the emergence of a new mission, yet it was during his enslavement in Ireland that he was shaped by God. He became someone who could endure trials and be fruitful despite challenges along the way. He described the process of his formation in this way:

> ...I remained on in Ireland, and that not of my own choosing, until I almost perished. However, it was very good for me, since God straightened me out, and he prepared me for what I would be today.[83]

Leadership formation continues to be of utmost importance today if we too are to become people who can persist in ministry. The 'clergy attrition rate' is substantial and it is usually suggested that more than 50% of those who enter Christian ministry leave within the first 10 years. The underlying reasons

---

[83] *Confessio* 28

for this loss and the factors involved are complex, but it is worth reflecting on the personal qualities needed to persevere in ministry.

The terms *adaptability* and *resilience* capture the essence of Patrick's life and ministry. As we saw in the case of Patrick, these characteristics are formed slowly, often in adversity, and they are gradually honed over time through repeatedly making good choices and learning from bad ones. There is, unfortunately, no such thing as instant maturity and no substitute for character formation in the development of Christian leaders.

Recently, I have had conversations with people involved in church planting forums and my impression is that there is much importance placed on the zeal and commitment of church planters. There is, however, little awareness of the potential benefits of something which, at first glance, seems quite unrelated, namely the value of solitude and silence (what we would now see as the basis for contemplative spirituality). These played a key role in Patrick's personal formation when he was a slave since it was in that context that he experienced a fuller life in the Spirit. Such practices may hold a key to longevity in ministry, particularly in times of transition and in situations of liminality. Patrick's early experience of discovering God in adversity radically shifted his focus, and he developed a new-found confidence as he prayed, heard the voice of the Spirit, and became grounded in Scripture.

As in the case of Patrick, formative experiences are rarely planned but come our way unbidden. Our response determines the outcome and, as the saying goes, facing adversity either makes us bitter or better. Slavery demanded that Patrick should develop great *adaptability* for the sake of survival, as he had no choice but to adapt to the adverse conditions in which he found himself. It was in that context that he both sought God and was, in turn, shaped by God to become the person he needed to be for his future ministry. Re-engaging with the Irish meant that he would have to employ the adaptability he had developed in order to face the challenges presented by the social and political realities encountered on his return to pagan Ireland.

We have also seen that Patrick exhibited *resilience* in response to the opposition he faced in Ireland as well as in responding to the negative reactions of many of his associates in Britain. His resilience was undoubtedly related to faith that was grounded in his personal experience of God's ability to act in whatever circumstances he faced. This confidence, combined with a clear sense that God had called and subsequently commissioned him, enabled Patrick to endure hostility and overcome the numerous obstacles encountered in the course of his ministry. God had formed within Patrick the resilience and adaptability he would need upon returning to Ireland. These qualities are also what we need in the context of a post-Christian West.

* * * * * * * *

In summary, it can be a challenge for church leaders to persevere in modern Western culture, particularly at those times when there is little external validation of our ministry. Patrick's story illustrates how the development of character attributes, such as resilience and adaptability, equip us for sustained leadership, enabling us to persist with enough engagement and for enough time to see fruit in the long term – fruit that will abide.

The formative experiences of Patrick's difficult early life gave rise to his utter dependence on the grace of God for both his personal situation and the outcome of his ministry. In captivity, he had reached the end of his ability to control the world around him, and this imbued him with the humility to

Culmination

recognise that whatever was achieved was by God's grace. He viewed the outcome of his ministry as a gift from God, certainly not dependent on any innate qualities which he himself possessed. It is fitting to end this chapter with Patrick's own words where he simply states that his impact was purely dependent on God. This closing statement of his *Confession*, sums up the spirit of Patrick in one short paragraph:

> I now pray for anyone who believes in and fears God who may perchance come upon this writing which Patrick, the sinner and unlearned one, wrote in Ireland. I wrote it so that no one could say that whatever little I did, or anything I made visible according to God's pleasure, was done in ignorance. Rather, you should judge the situation and let it be truly believed that it was the gift of God. And this is my declaration [confessio] before I die.

10

Conclusion

Patrick lived in an age of massive societal change. With the marginalisation of the Church in the early 5th century, the Church in Britain faced a slowly developing crisis. We saw that the incursion of pagan Angles, Saxons and Jutes from the near continent eventually resulted in the centre of Christianity being pushed to the more rural western fringes of the British Isles. In reaction to this situation of decline and marginalisation, it would have been easy for Patrick to lose heart, or even to abandon faith altogether. In such circumstances, there was little to encourage those who remained faithful to the true God, as it appeared that they were now on the losing side with the rising tide of paganism in evidence.

Yet God was not fazed by this situation, and he continued to act, albeit often in hidden ways and on the margins. Part of his response was to propel the young Patrick westward across the sea to the edge of the then-known world, to Ireland, into the pagan heartland, initially as a slave, having been abducted by pirate raiders. Christianity would eventually gain an incredibly strong foothold in Ireland. Amid adversity, God was on the move and, in time, this new centre of Christianity would give rise to wave upon wave of missionary activity spreading back to Britain, present-day Scotland and much of continental Europe. Who could have predicted that a missional movement would arise out of the disaster of Christianity's decline in 5th century Britain?

It has been suggested that the concept of liminality is a suitable lens through which to reflect on our own current situation in the West since increasingly discontinuous change has become an almost constant state. Our liminal experience creates discomfort and insecurity but it is, in fact, the perfect context to remind us of our need to listen for the voice of the Spirit and, consequently, it may actually provide the setting in which God is most likely to speak to us (or perhaps in which we are more likely to seek Him). We are living in an in-between space, a time of profound disorientation. Yet taking the long view, we can see this as simply a time of transition and disorientation which will at some point give way to reorientation. The challenge is to remain faithful, not lose heart, and to persist in our calling – a challenge met, in weakness and humility, but par excellence, by Patrick. His story can, therefore, instruct and inspire us today.

Patrick's Life as a Parable

[Jesus] was teaching them many things in parables.[84]

A parable is a story with an underlying meaning and like all good stories, parables work by engaging both our intellect and our emotion. They often communicate their message at a deeper level than prose might and as we 'get inside' a parable our imagination is stimulated.

Jesus never made it clear whether the parables he told were based on actual events, such as those we might find in Patrick's story, or whether he constructed purely imaginative narratives based on careful observation of people. I have treated Patrick's life as a form of parable to help us imagine –

---

[84] Mark 4:2

or reimagine - how leadership might look today. Patrick has stimulated my own imagination, and I hope that his story has done the same for you. Inspiration and imagination belong to the realm of the Spirit as well as being within the remit of Scripture, particularly the narrative sections, the Gospels and Acts, the Prophetic Books, and the Psalms. Although not on the same level as Scripture, stories such as Patrick's can act as historical parables for the modern day.

Parables help us to take a fresh look at our attitude towards God, other people and ourselves. They communicate values in memorable ways and, as stories, their affective impact remains with us and gradually shapes our attitudes and behaviour. For example, Patrick's description of himself as a sinner and the least of all Christians conveys more about real humility than an essay on the need for humility ever could.

When I studied theology, I was taught that a parable makes just one point, and that our task was to uncover and be able succinctly to summarise its underlying meaning. In fact, this process takes an imaginative story and turns it into something rather more cerebral! This so-called 'one point hypothesis' was first propounded by a theologian named Julicher. Understood in this way, Patrick's *Confession* is a parable about how God used an unworthy person, 'the sinner Patrick', to great effect.

Patrick's story does indeed illustrate this, portraying how God took an unlikely young man, changed his orientation in life and, despite an unpromising start in life, how he used Patrick to initiate a movement which was to last for hundreds of years. The main point is not that God can do *exactly* the same with us, but that *even though* our own lives may show little promise, *even though* we may disqualify ourselves from being used by God in such ways, and despite our bewilderment in finding ourselves in such an ever-changing context, there is in Patrick's story the hope that we too may find such grace operative in our own lives.

Conclusion

Several decades after discovering Julicher, and having re-engaged with formal theological study, I discovered that his method was now less popular and that a change in approach had taken place (one which appealed to me). The one-point hypothesis was no longer in fashion but was replaced by an emphasis on unearthing a whole variety of meanings that potentially could be seen in narratives such as parables. This was summed up in the phrase, 'the innate openness of stories' which implies that there are several truths to be discovered and that in seeking to understand their relevance for our lives we can legitimately let our imaginations roam more freely. This approach came with the caveat that we must not roam too far, since there are limits as to what any given story can possibly mean.

For example, The Parable of the Prodigal Son, under Julicher, teaches us about humanity's propensity for waywardness and our need to return to God. But seen through the lens of 'the innate openness of stories' this parable illustrates additional factors such as the destructive power of envy at work in the older brother, as well as the deep yearning of God for reconciliation as illustrated by the father embracing his lost and flawed son and, rather than castigating him, extravagantly celebrating his return.[85]

Adopting this more open approach to Patrick's life has brought into focus several different themes which have been explored, including the way in which adverse conditions are used to produce character; the fact that God uses us when we might actually disqualify ourselves; the need to engage with, rather than avoid, conflict; and the fact that our confidence needs to be based on the Word and the Spirit as well as on our call and commission for ministry. Yet it would be a mistake to regard these themes as a list to which we should aspire. As

---

[85] See: Henri Nouwen, *The Return of the Prodigal Son*. London, DLT, 1994.

mentioned, parables mostly do their work by engaging our imaginations rather than by creating a tick list which we must aim to fulfil. They enable us to view ourselves and our situation afresh by providing us with a new lens through which we can reframe the past, the present and the future.

Any attempt to turn such stories into a series of lessons to be applied destroys their innate power to effect change by transforming the way we see things. As such, they act in a similar way to some of Patrick's dreams, providing fresh direction, creating hope and instilling confidence. In this, the importance of our inner imaginative world is not to be underestimated. I suspect that once Patrick had heard the voice of the Irish calling him to walk among them once again, an image of his return to them formed in his mind and, once imagined, this unthinkable impossibility was actually rendered possible. Perhaps it could have been ignored but it couldn't be unimagined. Reflection on such aspects of Patrick's life enables us to reimagine our lives without resorting to formulaic, off-the-peg answers. The inspiration we gain from Patrick's story suggests that reliance on God himself is better than depending primarily on previously acquired knowledge, well-honed skills or even what has worked for us in the past.

Reimagining Church Leadership

We saw in the last chapter that Patrick's story highlights the vital necessity in liminal situations of adaptability and resilience, qualities that we too surely need in our time. Historical examples can also help us re-evaluate approaches to leadership which although helpful, or even vital, in a bygone age, are now less helpful in our current situation and context.

We often, in fact, continue doing things that are a hangover from the past but which have long surpassed their usefulness. This is sometimes described as 'the hierarchical promotion of ideas'. These established ways of doing things sometimes acquire almost hallowed status despite outliving their original value. Churches too sometimes perpetuate practices that were instituted for very sound reasons, but which can continue into time immemorial once the circumstances which led to their adoption in the first place have faded in the mists of time.

The challenge is to remain faithful to the ideas and values of Scripture but to realise when *traditionalism* has taken root. If we are to reimagine leadership for today this will involve going back to the source, primarily the Bible, and asking ourselves how we can remain faithful to the essence of biblical faith yet outwork it in our present context, a context very different from that of the New Testament. It is also worth noting that our current setting and situation differs from the cultural contexts in which most modern denominations were formed. This process of retrieval, first going back to the source, and then of renewal (re-imagining the specific situation currently faced) is not always easy. It is sometimes described using the French term *ressourcement,* implying both a return to the source as well as of modernisation and updating.

Patrick's ministry in Ireland aimed to create Church with a specific people group, in a particular place and in a specific cultural context. It required faithfulness to the tradition he had received but also flexibility and the willingness to do something new, outside the paradigm with which he had grown up. The idea that Roman civilisation, or its vestiges, was the main vehicle for the spread of the gospel was a sacred cow which needed to be slaughtered.

In the rapidly changing culture of the West and taking into account the specifics of our own locale, the challenge is to think through where we too need to apply the concept of *ressourcement*. It can be difficult to acknowledge when our practices have become outmoded and even more difficult to change familiar and, therefore, reassuring ways of doing things. Historical examples, particularly those drawn from the discipline of studying mission history, can help us to get a clearer focus on what is needed in our own time as, increasingly, we find ourselves in a missionary context.

Cultivating Hopefulness

> Each situation has its own temptations and challenges. In times of prosperity, the temptation is towards pride and arrogance. In times of adversity, the temptation is towards cynicism and despair. All are to be noticed and resisted.[86]

History illustrates the fact that we should expect the fortunes of the Church to wax and wane but, even so, situations of decline or of unforeseen challenges are nonetheless disorientating. Like Israel on entering the desert, our generation has not been this way before and the terrain is unfamiliar and uncharted. Yet we can soon become accustomed to the new situation and the danger is that we, like them, might wander endlessly in all-too-familiar circles.

How can we avoid cynicism and despair in such circumstances? Where can we look for stories to encourage, inspire and help us reimagine leadership? Reflecting on the lives of past figures to whom we might look, including Patrick, we see some patterns emerging:

1. GOD MAY WELL USE UNLIKELY PEOPLE

The young Patrick showed little interest in the Christian faith of his forebears. He was not the sort of keen Christian we might consider suitable for ministry and, rather like the young David,

---

[86] Aidan Ryan, *Pastoral Ministry in Changing Times*. Dublin, Messenger Publications, 2019, p.13.

he was an unlikely candidate on which to pin hope for the future. Furthermore, he was initially removed from any possibility of engagement, a mere slave with the expectation of lifelong servitude. There was very little about Patrick that would make us consider him suitable to spearhead a mission to the then pagan world and even once he had embarked on his mission, his chances of success, humanly speaking, were extremely poor. God can, of course, use those of us who are 'likely candidates' for ministry - those with evident skills, the right education and background – but it seems that God often selects the unlikely candidate such as a young unmarried woman, the son of a carpenter, or a 16-year-old slave with little attachment to Christianity. The God who chooses the weak things of this world to confound the strong is likely to surprise us with his choices again and again.

2. GOD'S ACTION MAY BE UNPREDICTABLE

Faced with the situation of the British Church at the beginning of the 5th century and asked to devise a strategy for the future of the Church, it is unlikely that we would have been enthusiastic about sending Patrick back to Ireland. We would never have predicted that, in the future, missionaries from Ireland would aid the re-evangelisation of Britain and beyond.

Attempting to second-guess what God might do is almost always unproductive. Patrick's peers were evidently as puzzled as we might have been when he persisted with his mission to the Irish. In a similar vein, Jesus' family considered his actions unwise, and they sought to persuade him that his chosen approach to his mission was misguided (Mark 3:21).

Our understanding, even when shaped by Scripture, can actually cloud our vision and we all too easily fail to perceive what God is doing. We need the Word (like never before) but we also need the Spirit to guide us and reveal where God is actually moving. In the days of the early church, the Sanhedrin was convinced that the apostles were up to no good. These were Bible-believing people whose concepts had been shaped by the Hebrew Scripture but, nonetheless, clearly they had missed the point. It took the intervention of Gamaliel to bring wisdom to bear, encouraging them to wait and observe the outcome of events before coming to a judgment (Acts 5:34-49).

Fortunately, Patrick relied on the voice of the Spirit, rather than on his own ideas or understanding, or even on the received wisdom of his peers. This enabled God to do some completely unpredictable but wonderful things, such as guiding him from slavery to freedom and subsequently calling him back to the place of his former captivity.

3. GOD MAY WELL USE THOSE WHOM WE FEEL ARE UNQUALIFIED

Patrick felt himself to be poorly qualified, a second-rate scholar (and what is more he had disqualified himself by an unnamed sin that his detractors had used to discredit him). Similarly, in the eyes of the chief priest and the elders, Jesus was uncredentialled and was seriously challenged about the source of his authority to perform miracles (Mark 11:28).

It is interesting to note that early Methodism was spearheaded by preachers who were 'laymen' placed in charge of class meetings and groups. John Wesley had been initially reluctant to use non-ordained persons, but rapid growth had actually made this a necessity. Relying on those with practical experience learned 'on the job' led to great success. The potential benefits of leaders today who lack more formal training but who are nonetheless competent is evidenced by research conducted in the UK:

> It is some of the non-institutional denominations which are growing. Who are these? In Britain they are mostly those who worship in borrowed premises (13% of

congregations in Britain have no building), and many have theologically untrained leadership who nevertheless perform very competently! [87]

These three adjectives – *unlikely*, *unpredictable*, and *unqualified* - are worth bearing in mind for our own day. Hope often emerges in unusual, unthought-of places, and it appears that in Patrick's day at the beginning of what would prove to be a time of increasing instability, disorientation and eventual Church decline in Britain, God was at work in unexpected ways and in an unexpected place. His unlikely strategy involved teaching a young slave boy to pray. Whilst not suggesting that planning is wrong, it would seem to be of paramount importance that before we create strategies of our own, we learn to identify where, in fact, God is already at work by His Spirit in the challenging situations we face and which surround us.

Leading in Times of Transition

> Everything has been figured out, except how to live.
> JEAN-PAUL SARTRE

We have seen that the underlying instability in society and the accompanying gathering momentum of paganism at home in Britain formed the context in which Patrick received his call to return to the Irish. His long period of preparation before returning suggests that he took seriously the magnitude of this task and the challenges he faced. We too must take the magnitude of the task we face seriously with sober appraisal and appreciation of the situation we currently experience in the West. How can we as leaders lead in such circumstances?

---

[87] https://static1.squarespace.com/static/54228e0ce4b059910e19e44e/t/639216fee4b18063da5b5587/1670518534279/FUTURE_FIRST_Issue+84+December+2022+v3.pdf

How can we earn respect in an age where, in Western society particularly, those in any kind of authority position might not be taken seriously or be subject to derision?

It is difficult to navigate a bewildering new terrain as the old maps – the way we used to lead – are not always a reliable guide to leadership in this uncharted territory. We knew how to lead the Church of 30 or 40 years ago, but our new landscape presents us with unprecedented challenges to which there are no easy answers. The sort of leadership that was optimal in the period sometimes referred to as 'Christendom' may no longer be effective or even viable today.[88] Something qualitatively different is called for to find a new way of being in the world, both for church leaders and the Church as a whole.

To misquote Sartre, 'We have figured everything out, *except how to lead*'. The transition in progress requires, for many, quite radical changes in style of leadership, one of which must surely include fostering the empowerment of all believers. Yet Patrick's life suggests that an even more fundamental issue is that of the personal formation of leaders themselves, particularly with regards to the development of character and the ability to keep in step with the Spirit. Patrick's story of hope, which arose in an unpromising situation, can act as a reminder to us that the Church in the West does have a future if we, like Patrick, actively trust God and respond to His voice.

The terms we have explored in this chapter - unlikely, unpredictable, and unqualified - introduce a certain degree of vulnerability in church leadership as reliance on God rather than on our own insight, analysis or ability is called for. This is where we find ourselves drawn again to the life of Patrick and to his trust in God, to his resilience in the face of difficulties,

---

[88] In some regions of the USA, despite the separation of Church and State, politicians have taken the views of the Church more seriously than is the case in Europe and this created what is in effect a Christendom-like situation.

opposition and unpopularity, and to his adaptability in the face of uncomfortable events and changes, both personal and cultural. He was willing to go to Ireland, and having formerly been *forced* to embrace vulnerability as a slave, was subsequently prepared to *freely* embrace vulnerability in response to God's call. Although such a move, based on obedience, represents the ultimate security of faith in God, in reality, it is likely in such demanding circumstances that we inevitably experience personal insecurity and, at times, feel out of our depth. Also, should God choose to use us, as in the case of Patrick, the voice of our own internal critic may ring loud and all too clear. But in God's hands these experiences of disorientation, insecurity and uncertainty are not wasted, but instead can be used as a suitable substrate for God to cultivate authoritative and effective leadership qualities in us.

It is this combination of vulnerability and authority forged through often bitter experience and difficulties over the long haul which characterised Patrick's life and ministry. His was, to quote Friedrich Nietzsche, 'a long obedience in the same direction' with no short cuts, nor necessarily any spectacular or easy answers. Perhaps paradoxically, given his position of relative powerlessness, it has been suggested that Patrick did not see himself as a mere representative of God but more as an ambassador. The authority he bore was nothing to do with wielding personal power but became almost innate, arising from his deepening dependence and trust in the power and authority of the God he served. Thomas O'Loughlin suggests that to encounter Patrick was to actually 'meet with Christ the judge' – weighty words indeed and ones that reflect the 'presence' and gravitas Patrick must have had.[89]

---

[89] O'Loughlin (1999), p.95.

Terminology

THE CELTS

The concept of 'the Celts' is much disputed by scholars. It is often used as a term to describe those peoples who traded with each other and who predominantly used the Atlantic Ocean as their main highway. In fact, there was no distinct ethnic grouping that could be referred to as being Celtic but rather a broad cultural 'colonisation' of certain regions with Celtic art, customs and religious practices spread through trade. At times, in this period, whole populations from one geographical area migrated to other far-flung regions.

Many authors use the term Celt in this way but here it is used to refer to those ethnic groups who spoke (or still speak) the Celtic languages. As Germanic and Roman languages became more widespread Celtic-speakers were eventually confined to Gaul (much of modern France), the western fringes of England, Wales and Scotland, as well as to the island of Ireland. These regions were somewhat sheltered from wider political and cultural forces at work in other parts of Europe and increasingly they became linked together by their particular expression of Christianity.

It is important to realise that those who spoke Celtic languages were never actually one single body of people, but that they had quite separate cultural and social identities.

Moreover, they would never have described themselves as being 'Celtic'. However, this is not in itself problematic since it is common for movements, groups, and historical periods to be identified and labelled in retrospect (they wouldn't have described themselves as living in the Dark Ages either!) The term 'Celt' is rather like the modern term 'European' – people in Sweden are culturally very different from those in Greece, yet there is a certain degree of commonality and shared values and, like those referred to as Celtic, there are distinct and particular confines to their geographical location.

THE CELTIC CHURCH

The second disputed term is 'Celtic Church'. Donald Meek, a self-confessed sceptic of the use of the term 'Celtic Church' rightly points out that it is preferable to refer to the Celtic *Churches* (plural) since local culture strongly influenced the shape and practices of regional churches such as those found in Wales, Scotland etc.[90] However, it can be argued that it is actually legitimate to use the term 'Celtic Church' as the churches in Celtic regions were often in contact with one another. In addition, they had certain common characteristics, in that, for example, they favoured a system of local leadership, abbots and abbesses, which existed alongside the more centralised system of bishops and archbishops which was more prominent elsewhere. Such common characteristics may well have existed for pragmatic rather than theological reasons and were related to their setting and local culture.

The Celtic Churches adhered to the distinctive value of pilgrimage which became a prominent feature of Celtic monasticism. Whereas we think of pilgrimage as visiting a holy

---

[90] Donald Meek, *The Quest for Celtic Christianity*. Edinburgh, Handsel Press, 2000, p.105.

site, they regarded it somewhat differently, in terms of going on a voyage of discovery, often to unfamiliar or inhospitable places. Sometimes this involved setting out with no clear destination in mind and trusting that God would show them where to go as they travelled.

It is only legitimate to speak of a 'Celtic Church' (or churches) with the proviso that they viewed themselves as being local expressions of a universal Church, not as separate entities and certainly never as one unified Celtic Church. Some prominent leaders were themselves ordained or even made bishops by the Pope and the presumed contrast between the Roman Church and the Celtic Church(es) has been greatly exaggerated. The fact that they hammered out of their differences at the Council of Whitby in 664 clearly indicates that they considered themselves to be part of the same entity as the Roman Church, rather than being distinctly Celtic.

SAINTS

This book is about a Celtic *saint*. In the New Testament the term 'saint' is used to describe all of us who are set apart for God's service, whatever our status or role in life. Elizabeth Rees points out that in the era of the Celtic saints: 'The term "saint" simply meant someone wise and holy, or any good Christian who had died'.[91] I am using the term in the same way, rather than as a title bestowed by the Church on especially gifted or sacrificial Christians. This first book focuses on Patrick with Finnian and Columba featuring subsequently. My selecting these particular saints is partly subjective in that I find them inspiring but also because they all have links with Ireland, and, particularly in the cases of Patrick and Columba, there are reliable sources of information about their lives.

---

[91] Elizabeth Rees, *Celtic Saints in Their Landscape*. Stroud, Amberley Publishing, 2011, p.7.

LEADERSHIP

I have tended to use the rather neutral term 'leader' in this book or to talk about ministry, rather than use terms such as clergy or pastor. This is because I want the book to have wide appeal and many in leadership roles in the church, mission agencies or in wider society relate less well to these more formal ecclesiastical terms. No judgment is implicated on the use of alternative terminology.

The drawback of using 'leader' is that it can conjure up visions of a church CEO (in management speak leaders are innovators and managers organisers). That is not my intention and although some church leaders are entrepreneurial, my use of the term here is different. 'Leader' is a catch-all term that implies someone who provides a degree of direction and goes before those led, rather like an Ancient Near Eastern shepherd walking ahead of his flock. Leaders do, in the jargon, 'cast a vision' but a vision of forming a community which develops empowered followers of Jesus who can serve those around them. The concept of leadership can apply whether church leaders adhere to a priestly model (as is found in episcopal churches), the 'pastor model' of non-conformity or the more entrepreneurial model common in some of the newer churches.

Further Reading

The following are suggestions for further reading for anyone wanting to explore some of the issues and topics covered in this book.

THE LIFE OF PATRICK

I have used three sources for Patrick's own writing. The first was the translation given in Oliver Davies, *Celtic Spirituality*.[92] Thomas O'Loughlin provided a very readable alternative in *Saint Patrick: The Man and his Work*.[93] Most quotations in this book come from the free online version of Patrick's *Confession* and his Letter that is available at Confessio.ie.[94] I have freely drawn on these versions of Patrick's writings. Muirchu's *Life* is found at Confessio.ie and in *Celtic Spirituality*. Michael Haykin has written an evangelical perspective on Patrick's ministry, *Patrick of Ireland: His Life and Impact*.[95]

I would also recommend the video on Patrick produced by CBN. This is an excellent docudrama with contributions

---

[92] Oliver Davies, *Celtic Spirituality*. New York, Paulist Press, 1999.

[93] Thomas O'Loughlin, *Saint Patrick: The Man and his Work*. London, SPCK, 1999.

[94] https://www.confessio.ie/etexts/confessio_english#

[95] Michael Haykin, *Patrick of Ireland: His Life and Impact*. Fern, Ros-shire, Christian Focus, 2014.

from some of the leading scholars in the field. [96]

THE CELTS

There are a number of books which I found very useful as an introduction to the topic of the Celts. Peter Berresford Ellis's book *A Brief History of the Celts* provides a good historical overview.[97] I am also a fan of the 'A Very Short Introduction' series published by Oxford University Press including the volume on the Celts. These are accessible and informative.

THE CELTIC CHURCH

When it comes to the Celtic Church, I would highly recommend starting with Ian Bradley's *Colonies of Heaven* and *Following the Celtic Way*.[98] 'Following' is a clever way of signalling that the author's previous book *The Celtic Way* contained material that needed revision. Anne Hughes has written a book intended for students, *The Celtic Church: Origins, Developments and Themes*. It is an excellent summary of much that is known concerning the Celtic Church.[99]

Two books which attempt to debunk some of the popular but largely inaccurate books on Celtic Christianity are Donald Meek's *The Quest for Celtic Christianity* and Marian Raikes' short book *Light from Dark Ages?*[100] These are well worth

---

[96] Available from CBN Films:
https://www.cbnfilms.com/iampatrick.php#:~:text=I%20AM%20PATRICK%3A%20The%20Patron,made%20a%20miraculous%20escape%20home.

[97] Peter Beresford Ellis, *A Brief History of the Celts*. London, Robinson, 2003.

[98] Ian Bradley, *Colonies of Heaven: Celtic Models for Today's Church*. London, DLT, 2000; Ian Bradley, Following the Celtic Way: A New Assessment of Celtic Christianity. London, DLT, 2018.

[99] Anne Hughes, *The Celtic Church: Origins, Developments and Themes*. Newtownards, Colourprint Educational, 2018.

[100] Donald Meek, The *Quest for Celtic Christianity*. Edinburgh, Handsel Press, 2000; Marian Raikes, *Light from Dark Ages? An Evangelical Critique*

reading for anyone wanting to delve more deeply into the topic and form their own opinion as to whether modern authors use or misuse history.

For those interested in Celtic monasticism, I would recommend Steven Vanderputten's *Medieval Monasticisms*.[101] Although the section on Irish monasticism is short, this masterpiece sets it in its wider context, demonstrating how the monasteries came to function as multi-purpose institutions and to exert much political power.

POPULAR BOOKS ON CELTIC CHRISTIANITY

Elizabeth Rees has written extensively on the topic of the saints such as *Celtic Saints in Their Landscape*, and *A Dictionary of Celtic Saints*.[102] These books are a light, easy read and although they present little in the way of critique of sources, they do provide some interesting background material.

There are very many popular books on Celtic spirituality which I have found helpful. Some need to be approached with caution, as they tend to conflate hagiography with history. This is particularly the case with those authors who rely on a collection of prayers and blessings dating to 19th century Scotland, the *Carmina Gadelica*. The *Carmina* is of great interest for that period, but it is not a reliable guide to early Celtic spirituality and readers need to be discerning in this respect.

I mentioned the myth that is perpetuated about the

---

of Celtic Spirituality. London, The Latimer Trust, 2012.

[101] Steven Vanderputten, *Medieval Monasticisms: Forms and Experiences of the Monastic Life in the Latin West*. Berlin, Walter de Gruyter GmbH, 2020.

[102] Elizabeth Rees, *Celtic Saints in Their Landscape*. Stroud, Amberley Publishing, 2011, and *A Dictionary of Celtic Saints*. Stroud, The History Press, 2012.

existence of a distinct monolithic Celtic Church. A similar construct that exists only in the mind of its supporters is that of a non-authoritarian Celtic Christianity. As we shall see in the second book in this series, in certain respects the Irish Church could be viewed as having been more authoritarian than, for instance, settings where the Rule of Benedict has been or is followed. With these caveats in mind, there is much that is stimulating in the more popular books on this topic.

About the Author

Richard lives in a small town in West Dorset, in the Southwest of England. He is married with three adult children and eight grandchildren. He is never happier than when he is in or near a river in some remote location with a fishing rod in hand. He is an amateur blues guitarist.

He has a background in General Practice (family medicine) as well as in psychotherapy and has been involved for 38 years in the leadership of two expressions of New Charismatic Churches, one a rural Community Church and currently a home-based church, The Meeting Place. Richard has also worked in theological education, having been Director of Studies for a Masters degree in Missional Leadership.

Richard is a trustee for the International Charismatic Consultation and formerly at Ffald y Brenin retreat centre in Wales. He is on the organising committee for the Gathering in Holy Spirit (Rome) and since 2012 has been involved in official Conversations between the New Charismatic Churches (non-denominational) and the Pontifical Council for Promoting Christian Unity in Rome. These involvements have resulted in many valued friendships and a growing awareness of the potential for Christians from different Church traditions to enrich one another's lives.

His recent publications include *The Characteristics of the New Charismatic Churches*, available on the Vatican website, and an article entitled *Networked Church: Theological, Sociological and Historical Perspectives* published in the journal Pneuma. In addition, he has published three books (see overleaf).

Email: finnianpress@icloud.com

You might also enjoy...

CULTIVATING GOD'S PRESENCE
Renewing Ancient Practices for Today's Church

This book introduces us to renewed patterns and rhythms for living which cultivate God's presence in our everyday lives. Inspired by accounts of Celtic monastics, Richard Roberts blends their example with personal experience and biblical insights to create an integrated approach to Christian living, fit for the twenty first century.

> *'There are few books that when I read, I don't want to put down, fewer still that when I have read, I want to read all over again. This is one such book.'*
> -ANNE DE LEYSER, LOCAL HOUSES OF PRAYER (FFALD Y BRENIN)

REDEEMING PROPHECY
A Practical Guide to Authentic Prophetic Ministry

REDEEMING PROPHECY evaluates the practice of prophecy in today's Church using the lens of Scripture and of church history.

> *'A great book on prophecy. I found it helpful, practical, and an easy quick read of only about 150 pages.'*
> -DR RANDY CLARK (GLOBAL AWAKENING)

AVAILABLE FROM AMAZON, BARNES & NOBLE, WATERSTONES

www.ingramcontent.com/pod-product-compliance
Lightning Source LLC
LaVergne TN
LVHW011839060526
838200LV00054B/4100